LIKE A ROOT
OUT OF DRY GROUND

LIKE A ROOT
OUT OF DRY GROUND

Reflections and resources for Holy Week
and Easter from the Iona Community

Neil Paynter (ed)

wild goose
publications

www.ionabooks.com

First published 2024 by
Wild Goose Publications
Suite 9, Fairfield, 1048 Govan Road, Glasgow G51 4XS, Scotland
the publishing division of the Iona Community.
Scottish Charity No. SC003794. Limited Company Reg. No. SC096243.

ISBN 978-1-80432-326-7
Cover image © Lovelyday12 | Dreamstime.com

Overseas distribution
Australia: Willow Connection Pty Ltd, 1/13 Kell Mather Drive,
Lennox Head, NSW 2478
New Zealand: Pleroma, Higginson Street, Otane 4170, Central Hawkes Bay

Printed in the UK by Page Bros (Norwich) Ltd

CONTENTS

INTRODUCTION

Someone once said to me that what they appreciate about books like this is all the different voices. Reading collections like this, they said, helped them to feel part of 'a little community of hope'. In 2024, we all need hope.

The readings and resources here were written by members, associates and friends of the Iona Community. Thank you so much to everyone who contributed to this book.

Each day of Holy Week follows the same sort of rhythm: Bible reading, reflection, prayer, meditation/questions. The Bible readings are taken from the *Revised Common Lectionary*.

May this book accompany you on your journey through Holy Week, and beyond. May it help you to feel part of a community of hope.

> *'And now I would like to invite you to imagine hard ground – a pavement or concrete. Or dry desert floor, cracked and hard. Imagine it in as much detail as you can: how it looks, the colours, how it would feel beneath your feet or if you touched it with your palm. Maybe imagine how it would smell.*
>
> *Then imagine a plant breaking through the hard ground.*
>
> *Imagine the strength and resilience of the plant as it grows tiny bit by bit, pushing against the resistance of the soil or concrete.*
>
> *Imagine how it comes out into the light and air.*
>
> *Imagine it spreading its roots and opening its leaves.*
>
> *Imagine it growing and perhaps forming a flower bud and opening a flower.*
>
> *Imagine how that might feel.*
>
> *Now think of a situation where life is hard, where there's injustice, exclusion and oppression and people need to break through like the plant. A situation where resistance and resilience are needed. Then think of how you could support these people. Then go out and do it!'* (Urzula Glienecke)

Neil Paynter, Christmas 2023

Palm Sunday

What does it mean to be blessed by God?

Emma Major

Bible readings

O give thanks to the LORD, for he is good;
  his steadfast love endures forever!

Let Israel say,
  'His steadfast love endures forever.' …

Open to me the gates of righteousness,
  that I may enter through them
  and give thanks to the LORD.

This is the gate of the LORD;
  the righteous shall enter through it.

I thank you that you have answered me
  and have become my salvation.
The stone that the builders rejected
  has become the chief cornerstone.
This is the LORD's doing;
  it is marvellous in our eyes.
This is the day that the LORD has made;
  let us rejoice and be glad in it.
Save us, we beseech you, O LORD!
  O LORD, we beseech you, give us success!

Blessed is the one who comes in the name of the LORD.
  We bless you from the house of the Lord.
The LORD is God,
  and he has given us light.
Bind the festal procession with branches,
  up to the horns of the altar.

You are my God, and I will give thanks to you;
  you are my God, I will extol you.

O give thanks to the LORD, for he is good,
  for his steadfast love endures forever.

Psalm 118:1–2,19–29 (NRSV)

… they brought the colt to Jesus and threw their cloaks on it; and he sat on it.

Many people spread their cloaks on the road, and others spread leafy branches that they had cut in the fields.

Then those who went ahead and those who followed were shouting, 'Hosanna! Blessed is the one who comes in the name of the Lord!

Blessed is the coming kingdom of our ancestor David! Hosanna in the highest heaven!'

Mark 11:7–10 (NRSV)

Reflection

'Blessed is the one who comes in the name of the Lord': a phrase so familiar to us, so full of love and peace, a statement of love of Jesus.

Yet these words, shouted by the crowds welcoming Jesus into Jerusalem, were more of a political statement than a thanksgiving to God. The crowd was declaring that Jesus was the saviour of Israel; they were welcoming the man who they believed would release them from the ruling Romans and transform their lives.

The crowd knew what they were declaring; they were quoting the words of Psalm 118:26.

They were rejoicing that God would triumph in their fight for their freedom. They believed that this was the start of their success, which over the generations they had come to doubt would ever come. They were celebrating that their lives would be transformed for the better.

Triumph
Freedom
Transformation
Success

These are not words which I associate with Jesus. These are not words of peace, reconciliation, justice, blessing or love.

And of course many people need these things, especially the downtrodden and oppressed, but most of us who are reading this today are blessed in our lives.

And so this Palm Sunday I wonder what we mean when we say 'Blessed is the name of the Lord'.

When we ask for God's blessings, what are our expectations?

Are we hoping for the same personal gifts as those who welcomed Jesus?

Do we long to triumph over others?
Do we ask for freedom from those who lead us?
Do we seek that sort of transformation in our lives?
Do we hope and pray for success?

There is nothing wrong with these words in the right context; we can triumph in our fight against dictators and seek freedom for those who are oppressed; we can ask God to help us be transformed in our lives for good, and pray for success in following God more closely.

But ... if we pray these words purely for the improvement of our own situations, then are we really joining Jesus in his care for the world?

I am blessed in my life. I have a roof over my head, a family who love me and food and water to sustain me. I give thanks every day for God's blessings. I am also disabled and ill and I long to be transformed physically and freed of my daily pain; but so much more than that, I pray to God for those who are not as blessed as I am in my life.

I try to follow Jesus' example to care for the poor, fight against injustice and love my enemy. This is what Jesus stood for as he rode the donkey into Jerusalem.

As we move from the period of Lent into Holy Week, we start to prepare for the great sadness of Good Friday, and the celebration of Easter Day. We take this journey every year, the same yet different, depending on our own situations and those in the world around us. Yet the one constant is that we will journey with Jesus, accompanied by the song of the people: 'Blessed is he who comes in the name of the Lord.'

So I wonder:

- What does it mean to be blessed by God?

- Do we doubt God when our prayers aren't answered?

- Do we remain steadfast in our love of God when our lives are not as we hoped?

- What does it mean to be a blessing to other people?

- Do we ask God to help us to help others?

- How can we be more like Jesus in our words and actions?

Blessed is the name of the Lord who loves the world beyond measure. Let us pray to be led to places where we can bless others as God has blessed us.

Prayer

God of light,
be with us in the dark times.
When we struggle to see the way,
help us to feel your comfort ever with us,
to know our worth in the world,
to hear your voice leading us each day,
to praise you as we emerge hopefully into safety.

Remind us to celebrate your love that knows no end
and to transform that celebration into action
for those less blessed than ourselves.
Blessed is Jesus who comes in the name of the Lord.
Amen

God, your love endures
bringing comfort in my fear.
I give praise in thanks.

(Haiku, Psalm 118)

MONDAY OF HOLY WEEK

Seeing hope in times of darkness

by Jimi and Julaine Calhoun

Bible reading

Thus says God, the LORD,
*   who created the heavens and stretched them out,*
*   who spread out the earth and what comes from it,*
who gives breath to the people upon it
*   and spirit to those who walk in it:*
I am the LORD; I have called you in righteousness;
*   I have taken you by the hand and kept you;*
I have given you as a covenant to the people,
*   a light to the nations,*
*   to open the eyes that are blind,*
to bring out the prisoners from the dungeon,
*   from the prison those who sit in darkness.*

Isaiah 42:5–7 (NRSV)

Reflection

This section of Isaiah sends a reminder that it was God who spread 'out the earth and what comes from it'. In light of today's environmental and social problems, it should be axiomatic that, as a people of faith and spiritual practice, we are to engage in activities to facilitate a better future on earth, and what comes from it, for everyone.

Biblical righteousness refers not only to individualistic morality, as it is commonly understood in many Christian circles, but also to larger, public notions of justice. As a result, justice is not a secondary priority in the gospel of Christ. Righteousness is in operation when God's justice is being carried out via our involvement in right living amidst the chaos of the human story.

In order to do this, we 'look to Jesus' to keep our vision clear, and then love every person who enters into our world equally. That is tough to do, but it becomes easier when we intentionally strive to see others as God sees them. This can only happen if we live each day with our spiritual eyes wide open. What follows serves as an example of a way our eyesight can become blurry:

One of our ministry partners was scheduled to travel to Spain. Two weeks before the scheduled departure date it was discovered that surgery was needed to repair a detached retina.

The retina senses light and sends signals to the brain, enabling a person to see. When your retina separates from the tissues that support it, it loses its blood supply, which transports nutrients and oxygen to the retina. This condition affects a person's vision and can lead to blindness.

That is similar to what happens when we separate ourselves from the Spirit. We lose the ability to see what really matters to God. Our Bible passage implies that nations, like individuals, can also suffer from this type of impaired vision.

Points to consider

At the beginning of the last century, a group of German psychologists developed theories about how people come to see the world around them called gestalt. They proposed that the human brain is programmed to perceive structure, shapes and patterns through logic, and this helps us make sense of our world. Our Bible reading leads us to a different conclusion. And that is, rather than relying on psychological insights to guide our vision, we should trust the Spirit to reveal what is worth seeing.

Proverbs 4:25 says it this way: 'Let your eyes look directly forward and your gaze be straight before you.'

The following are some initiatives that we could look into this Holy Week to help establish the reign of God and advance the common good:

- We could look into reforestation, regenerative farming and sustainable development programmes as potential solutions to global poverty.

- We could look into restorative justice as a replacement for retributive justice to subvert the type of incarceration that not only punishes the offender, but devastates the offender's family as well. This type of 'bringing out the prisoners' might require an end to reacting to anti-social behaviour with a collective anti-social response, and then replacing it with pro-social programmes.

- We could look into being more compassionate and accepting of others who are different, regardless of how those differences appear. This means rejecting the prevailing mindset that reduces people we disagree with to the level of a resented enemy.

Our Bible reading acknowledges the reality that there is a covenant between God and us, as well as between us and each other. This week is also called Passion Week. A passion for Christ inspires anticipation and enthusiasm. This is a time when we can and should become enthusiastic about our spiritual lives. Spiritual stagnation causes entropy, leading to rot and decay, which is a form of death. Holy Week concludes with Jesus' triumph over physical death. The Easter story is a model for us to rise above the type of death that is presently occurring in our social and environmental systems, for the benefit of all.

Prayer

Eternal and ever-present God, as we meditate on the wonder of your creation as it is in heaven and is to be on earth, open our eyes to perceive you; by your Spirit, realign our minds to believe you, and reawaken our hearts to receive you.

Let your presence fill our hearts and overflow in our actions. Lord, let the fire of your goodness and justice burn into us and through us that we may strive to transform the unjust structures of society.

Guide us in your wisdom to care for all of your creation. Interrupt us when we get caught up in our own complacency.

Alert us when our blindness results in caring only for our own. Expand our view to see that we all belong to you and to each other as one in you. Amen

Tuesday of Holy Week

Losing your life to find it

Martin Wroe

Bible reading

'Very truly, I tell you, unless a grain of wheat falls into the earth and dies, it remains just a single grain; but if it dies, it bears much fruit. Those who love their life lose it, and those who hate their life in this world will keep it for eternal life …'

John 12:24–25 (NRSV)

Very truly I reply to you, Jesus of Nazareth, sometimes I'm not quite sure what your point is. Unless … that is your point. Which might explain why your words have hung about in the way they have, while those of your contemporary troubadour-rabbi-poet-mystic-guru types have proven less historically sticky.

As Matthew, one of your early biographers, recalled, 'Jesus spoke all these things to the crowd in parables; he did not say anything to them without using a parable.'

In my mind's eye I see John, another of those biographers, looking at some notes he's been passed by someone who said they'd heard from someone who'd been listening to you speak one day. And how, that night, they had scratched down some lines. Lines about loving your life and losing it, or hating your life and keeping it for ever.

'Hating your life?'

Flicking through the singular collection of parables and poems that ended up being called 'Gospels', I sometimes have a suspicion that a particular utterance reflects the local unconscious bias of one of your editors. The kind of hang-up or hidden agenda that we all obliquely harbour.

But then, in another Gospel, that same thought seems to be repeated slightly differently, almost as if you were gradually drafting a poem, thinking aloud as you slowly found what it was you wanted to say.

The way Matthew's Gospel has you saying, 'Those who find their life will lose it, and those who lose their life for my sake will find it.'

Or Luke recalls you musing, 'For those who want to save their life will lose it, and those who lose their life for my sake will save it.'

As I think of you as someone who believed in the wisdom found in company, that a truth is often born in community, I also like to imagine you shared your first drafts with your friends.

Can I run this line past you, Mary M?

– Of course, Jesus, is it that one with the clause about 'hating your life in this world'?

It is actually.

– Have you dropped it yet?

I thought it had a little bit of a wow factor, to keep people interested.

– Well, as I think Martha and I both suggested yesterday, that won't resonate with those of us who don't hate our lives and don't plan to, despite all the hassle on the bad days. In fact it may well annoy us.

OK.

– Also …

Also?

– Remember what we said about compression?

You said it might help if I could abbreviate some of these ideas.

– We did.

Let me have another go.

– I'm here most days.

Losing your life to find it.

Is this the paradoxical notion that inspired Francis in the 13th century to turn his back on prosperity for a life of poverty? *(Can I be honest with you, Jesus? I know I can. That seems a little too much for me. Honestly? Between us … it's not going to happen.)*

Is it the climate activist who risks jail time by chaining themselves to others, halting the traffic, on a busy main road?

Or the one who takes the train not the plane? The halloumi not the bacon?

Is it the life of small decisions that build up over time, or the life of the big moment on the road to Damascus? Or Dagenham.

Is it the medical doctor who chooses to live and work in the place where she will no longer know the prospect of upward mobility? Or is it the parent losing the life they'd been looking forward to, to look after the parent who once raised them?

Or to care for a partner, now unexpectedly changed from the person they once chose to share a life with.

Is it remaining true to who you are even if your friends walk away from you and no one will stand up for you?

Is it a week which begins in the spotlight of popular acclaim and ends in the dismal defeat of betrayal?

Very truly, you've got me wondering.

Perhaps, as every life is different, every way we choose to lose our life will also be different.

And every way we find it.

***

It's not easy to lose your life
Without becoming dead
But it's still worth trying
In order to really find
Yourself

It's not easy to find there's
No such thing as an individual
But maybe it's worth the effort
To find yourself in
Others

It's not easy to accept that
None of us really exists
Except when we exist for each other
But why live only for yourself
When you might as well be dead?

It's not impossible to gain a whole world
In the frantic chase for everything
But what can you do with a world
If you lost your soul
while colonising it?

It's not easy to accept that
'I am because you are'
And that unless you are, I am not
But it is a pearl of great price
That day when you find your heart
In tune with the universe

It's not easy to lose your life
But until we try
How will we ever know about
The life we might find?

***

Who do you think of when you think of someone who has lost their life and found it?

Has there been a time when this was true for yourself?

What would it mean to 'hate' your life?

Are there times when you think, 'I wouldn't have put it like that, Jesus.'?

WEDNESDAY OF HOLY WEEK

The betrayal of Jesus

Kathy Galloway

Bible reading

After saying this Jesus was troubled in spirit, and declared, 'Very truly, I tell you, one of you will betray me.'

The disciples looked at one another, uncertain of whom he was speaking.

One of his disciples – the one whom Jesus loved – was reclining next to him; Simon Peter therefore motioned to him to ask Jesus of whom he was speaking.

So while reclining next to Jesus, he asked him, 'Lord, who is it?'

Jesus answered, 'It is the one to whom I give this piece of bread when I have dipped it in the dish.' So when he had dipped the piece of bread, he gave it to Judas son of Simon Iscariot.

After he received the piece of bread, Satan entered into him. Jesus said to him, 'Do quickly what you are going to do.'

Now no one at the table knew why he said this to him.

John 13:21–28 (NRSV)

Reflection

I was five years old. I was in Primary One, in a class with forty other five-year-olds. I got into a fight with a boy called Gordon. (I still remember his surname, but I'm not writing it here.) I have no recollection of why we were fighting; perhaps it was just because I had grown up in a remote house outside a rural village, and I had never been to a nursery or playgroup, and only had a little brother who was a toddler. Moving to the city must have been a bit of a shock, so perhaps I just wasn't very socialised.

Anyway, I hit Gordon, and he immediately started to wail. The teacher, who was writing on the blackboard and did not see the fight, turned round, saw and heard the commotion and asked sharply what was going on. Immediately, a dozen children were eager to answer 'Kathryn hit Gordon'. Gordon continued to sob as the teacher asked him what had happened, and he confirmed through his tears that indeed 'Kathryn hit me'.

You should know that there was another girl in the class called Kathryn (I still remember her surname too, but I'm not writing it here). She was a quiet little girl, hardly spoke and never answered any of the teacher's questions. I have no idea whether the teacher thought that she was a more likely suspect in the assault on Gordon. I cannot remember whether she protested her innocence, though I think it's possible that other children may have said that it wasn't her. All I remember is that the other Kathryn got the strap for my misdeed (mid-century Edinburgh was not very enlightened when it came to the corporal punishment of five-year-olds). And I said nothing. I did not own up. I did not confess my wrongdoing. I did not then, or at any later time, say sorry to either Gordon or Kathryn.

I have felt guilty about this incident for my whole life. I knew that I had done wrong. Not so much for hitting Gordon, but for letting the other Kathryn take the blame, and the punishment, instead of me. I didn't have words for it back then, but now (and for many years) I see that it was a great act of betrayal.

Thinking about it, it was of course a betrayal of the innocent Kathryn. It was also a betrayal of my parents, who would not have been at all happy with me for my failure to own up (my five-year-old sin of omission!). And it was a betrayal of myself, because I clearly knew very well even then the difference between right and wrong, or at least, between what was fair and what was unfair. And perhaps I have felt it for so long as a betrayal of the truth.

Would that all our betrayals were possessed of such simple moral clarity. It would make it so much easier to know who to blame (which is, let's face it, more often our concern than acknowledging where we are the ones at fault). In reality, our betrayals are far more often a gradual accumulation of small deceits, disappointments and frustrations, of unhappy compromises and unmet ideals.

And what is true of personal betrayals, our own or others, is also true of the collective betrayals we are part of, simply by our existence as citizens of our country, as members even of the human race. We are all of us born into complicity, part of an oppressive, dehumanising world order for which we did not give our permission, and from which it is very hard to dissent, even when we try.

But the discourse around these betrayals are so often unedifying, providing neither justice, hope nor healing for those who have been betrayed by friends, by churches, by empires, nor hope and transformation for those who have placed themselves in the role of betrayer.

Some words from Robert Louis Stevenson's Christmas Sermon seem apt here ...

> *'... the truth is, that all these interventions and denunciations and militant mongerings of moral half-truths, though they be sometimes needful, though they are often enjoyable, do yet belong to an inferior grade of duties. Ill-temper and envy and revenge find here an arsenal of pious disguises; this is the playground of inverted lusts. With a little more patience and a little less temper, a gentler and wiser method might be found in almost every case; and the knot that we cut by some fine heady quarrelscene in private life, or, in public affairs, by some denunciatory act against what we are pleased to call our neighbour's vices, might yet have been unwoven by the hand of sympathy ...'* [1]

The betrayal of Jesus by Judas was a terrible violation of friendship that had been formed over three years of walking together. It was indicated in a context of great intimacy and great danger, of sharing the Passover feast with this little, fragile community. We cannot know why Judas sold Jesus out to the authorities. Perhaps he was an agent of the Roman Empire. Perhaps he was an impatient revolutionary, frustrated by the failure of Jesus to lead a political uprising. Perhaps he just did it for the money! There are plenty of theories. In any event, it didn't end well for Judas. Overcome by shame, he killed himself.

John's Gospel tells us that Jesus was troubled in spirit because he intuited this imminent betrayal. Clearly he knew that the act would set in motion a series of events that he could not control; 'do it quickly' he said to Judas. He did not attempt to stop him. He did not alert the others to Judas's intended treachery. He initiated no violence, and subsequently, when the betrayal and arrest actually happened, he prevented Peter's violent defence of him, and addressed Judas as 'Friend'.

And thereafter, through all his suffering, his pain and his self-doubt, he remained centred in the same spirit of love and faithful friendship that had marked his whole ministry till his final breath.

Prayer

O Christ our enlightener,
once and for all,
you broke the link between suffering and punishment,
erased the line between deserving and undeserving
and invited the unseeing to open their eyes
to the truth about themselves.
Doing this, you revealed yourself,
became vulnerable.
Preserve us from the defendedness that makes us vicious,
give us insight to see the structures of injustice by which we profit,
and grace to cherish all people in our vulnerability,
knowing that we all live within your love.

For further reflection

As people who have both endured and inflicted the violence of betrayal, and as we seek to live in the spirit of love and friendship, we might like to read and reflect on Hebrews 12:1–3, which is one of the set texts for Wednesday of Holy Week.

Note:

1. Robert Louis Stevenson, *Christmas Sermon*, 1900

MAUNDY THURSDAY

'Any questions?'

Katharine M. Preston

Bible reading

'I give you a new commandment, that you love one another. Just as I have loved you, you also should love one another. By this everyone will know that you are my disciples, if you have love for one another.'

John 13:34–35 (NRSV)

Reflection

'A new command I give you: Love one another. As I have loved you, so you must love one another.

Any questions?'

Seems straightforward. So why aren't we better at doing it?

I looked up 'maundy'. It was a revelation to me that it is from the Old French *mande*, in turn from the Latin *mandatum*, which means 'mandate or command'.

So, on Maundy Thursday, how come we kind of dance around the commandment that should be at the very centre of our faith?

Some of us give in to our longing to reconstruct the atmosphere of belonging in the upper room that night, trying to sort of be there, with Jesus. Inspired by Jesus' demonstration of humble service, we get caught up in a re-enactment of the foot-washing that happens just before he gives this commandment to his disciples. Or we bathe in the gentle beauty of that last meal, where the template for our ongoing Eucharistic sharing is established, inviting us to consume bread and wine at the Lord's table.

Or we look ahead to the next day and make preparations.

I worshipped with the Episcopal (Anglican) Church for many years. On Maundy Thursday, there was a 'stripping of the altar', the removal of *everything* from the sanctuary: ornaments, linens, candles, even the cross. A version of this is done at Iona Abbey on Thursday of Holy Week: liturgical items are carried out, and the table, font, pulpit are draped in black.

I always thought the stripping away of any ornamentation in the sanctuary on Maundy Thursday was performed simply as a precursor to Good Friday:

basically, a housecleaning to get the church ready for the Horrible Thing To Come the next day.

Re-enactment or preparation, in either case, the central commandment is ignored: 'LOVE one another. As I have loved you, so you must love one another.'

Maundy Thursday has nothing to do with the presence or absence of churchly accoutrements or the re-enactment of foot-washing or even the commemoration of a meal at the Lord's table. If anything – it should be a clearing of the decks of our *hearts*, so to make room for the central commandment that Jesus gives to his disciples and, by extension, us that night.

There is more:

'By this everyone will know that you are my disciples, if you love one another.'

So, what does that look like?

No tattoos, no secret handshakes, no special-coloured T-shirts, no red baseball caps?

Try to imagine identifying a community of people by watching how much they *love one another.*

What does it feel like to be a part of such a community?

It sounds like very hard work, so we dance around it again. Easier to evoke some exegesis that says that the version in the Gospel of John of the 'new commandment' should be interpreted as referring *only* to those who were in the room *physically* with him that night: 'Love one another (i.e., the disciples present) as I have loved you.'

Might that get us off the hook?

Or we might say to ourselves, surely, he is simply admonishing us to love those in our present worshipping circle, in the pews next to us, or fellow Iona Community members, associates and friends. Easy to love those with whom I share a commitment to justice, peace and the integrity of creation.

But: 'Show us this day whom we must love', challenges the *Iona Abbey Worship Book* in a prayer.[1]

And, in other gospels, it is made clear that the commandment to love one another extends not only to those in our worshipping communities, but to neighbours we might not know, and even to 'enemies', people who really do think and act differently from us.

So, when Jesus commands us 'to love one another', is he talking about those in my town and country who would support an authoritarian regime that would put millions of immigrants in camps before widespread deportation; use the U.S. military for domestic law enforcement against demonstrators; promote the use of fossil fuels here and abroad; rescind regulations prohibiting discrimination on the basis of sexual identity; and restructure the Executive branch of government so that political enemies could be punished?[2]

Really? Love those people?

When Jesus commands us to 'love one another', is he talking about people who kill out of hate, fear and revenge? Is he talking about the leaders of Hamas? Is he talking about the extreme right in the government of Israel and the settlers in the West Bank?

Yes.

'Any questions?'

Prayer

Well, yes, dear, challenging God, I do have questions …

You know my heart, that I do not *hate* people; even as I hate their actions.

But when You call on me, no, *command* me, to 'love' people who say they hate others, who would hurt others, I could use some help.

Help me move beyond lip-service prayer on this. To acknowledge these people, to 'see' them.

Help me move beyond just pity for them. Beyond just excusing their actions because I know that rage and fear and revenge are bending their very souls.

Help me see something in them that we have in common, so that they become actually *precious* to me (as they are to You).

Help me be part of a community that incriminates itself as being followers of Jesus because of the way we love.

Help me clear out my heart of all the world-weary impediments of doubt and cynicism and fear so there is space for that Love.

In the name of that embodied Love.

Amen

Questions/actions

What *specific* characteristics do you see when you observe a community loving each other as Jesus loves us?

Write a 'love' letter to, or better still try to start a conversation with, someone with whom you seem to disagree on everything. If it is a politician (a likely choice, I am guessing) try to find *something* you admire in them, something in their vision for your community that you share with them.

Be prepared to listen. (A good symptom of love, I think.)

Notes:

1. From a prayer for Monday morning, *Iona Abbey Worship Book*, Wild Goose Publications, 2001
2. These items are enumerated in Project 2025, a careful plan being developed for after the 2024 U.S. presidential election by the Heritage Foundation, a conservative U.S. think tank.

GOOD FRIDAY

God's servants

Urzula Glienecke

Bible reading

See, my servant shall prosper;
   he shall be exalted and lifted up,
   and shall be very high.
Just as there were many who were astonished at him
   – so marred was his appearance, beyond human semblance,
   and his form beyond that of mortals –
so he shall startle many nations;
   kings shall shut their mouths because of him;
for that which had not been told them they shall see,
   and that which they had not heard they shall contemplate.

Who has believed what we have heard?
   And to whom has the arm of the LORD been revealed?
For he grew up before him like a young plant,
   and like a root out of dry ground;
he had no form or majesty that we should look at him,
   nothing in his appearance that we should desire him.
He was despised and rejected by others;
   a man of suffering and acquainted with infirmity;
and as one from whom others hide their faces
   he was despised, and we held him of no account.

Surely he has borne our infirmities
   and carried our diseases;
yet we accounted him stricken,
   struck down by God, and afflicted.
But he was wounded for our transgressions,
   crushed for our iniquities;
upon him was the punishment that made us whole,
   and by his bruises we are healed.

Isaiah 52:13–53:5 (NRSV)

Reflection

Recently someone had left some small booklets at the Chaplaincy of the University of Edinburgh where I work. They stated the same message that I used to believe, that Jesus died for our sins:

'God created the world. People sinned and because of that were cut off from God. Therefore, we deserved to die and go to Hell for all eternity. Jesus died and paid for our sins on the Cross. Believe that and be saved!'

I do not believe that message any more. I do believe that God lovingly created the world – the universe, the Earth and all living beings. Including us, humans. I believe that God was behind and within the natural processes of the universe expanding and the evolution developing in marvellous and diverse ways. But I do not believe that Jesus paid for our sins by his suffering and death on the cross. For one – to whom would he have paid? To the Devil? I do not believe that there is a personalised evil. The evil is in our choices, the greed and the violence that we, humans, perpetrate. It's in the choices that we make and do not make. It's in our oppressing of other human beings and in our destroying of the very planet we live on.

Did Jesus pay it to God then? What kind of God would that be?! Someone demanding the torture, suffering, humiliation and death of God's own Son to pay for being 'offended by our sins', as it was thought for centuries? That is an image of a feudal lord and not of the God we meet and get to know in Jesus' life and teaching.

Now I believe that Jesus died because his life and teaching were uncomfortable for people, and they killed him. He died *because* of our sins, not *for* our sins. I believe that God came to the Earth, to us, because God wanted to be with us. God wanted to be one of us and to share our joy and pain, our lives, and our future. Jesus, God With Us started a movement, an avalanche of change. Well, probably he didn't start it, it was already there. As every missionary with an open heart and mind discovers that God is already there and at work in the world, so God was already there with us before Jesus was born into this world. God was in nature and all of creation; God was in the wisdom and compassion of the people of the Hebrew Bible, but also in other cultures, religions and stories. God was in the hand extended in friendship across differences; God was in kindness and generosity shown to a stranger, and in many, many more places and situations.

And Jesus came into this world as a vulnerable, helpless babe. He was born in a manger because there was no place for him in the inn. He became a refugee, because there was a threat of violence and death planned for him by a despotic ruler.

Like the servant described in Isaiah he grew up like a plant breaking through hard, dry ground. He was oppressed, despised, and killed in the end. But he was also loved. He brought the message of freedom for captives, equality for different genders, with justice and peace rooted in it. Jesus taught and lived a message that was full of hope for those oppressed and treated unequally. It was a message that was disturbing, uncomfortable and even threatening to those who held the lion's share of power and wealth, those in political and religious leadership. And that is why they killed him.

Reading the texts for Good Friday in the lectionary – John chapters 18 and 19, but also about the servant in Isaiah 52–53 and the lament in Psalm 22, no matter if it's about Jesus as it was often traditionally believed or not – my heart swells with love for such a person. I am thinking particularly of Jesus, but also of many others. How people who are treated the same way as the servant in Isaiah often bring so much, even change the world. People who are seen as lowly and without agency, people who are thought to have nothing to give often give the most. At times little things that are so important.

Allow me to tell you some real-life stories – stories from my life:

- There is a man who begs on the streets on my way to work. Let's call him Paul. He greets everyone who passes him with heartfelt friendliness and if they want – a conversation. He blesses me every time and asks how my long Covid is. He has never taken anything I have offered him. I feel heartened and invigorated every time we talk, no matter how hard the day has been.

- Another of my 'daily saints' is a man who could hardly speak. It was raining and I was tired. He ran after me and tried to tell me something. It seemed very important to him. Others who worked with him then explained to me that he wanted me to take his umbrella. That warmed my heart – and kept me dry too!

- And Auntie Anna in Latvia – she didn't know when she was born, not even the year. She had worked as a living bed warmer as a child and lived a simple, humble life mending socks for others. She encouraged me to study theology and to become a minister in the church. She told me: 'You are Maria, and your place is to sit at Jesus' feet and learn. Don't let that be taken away from you because you are a woman!'

- A young woman, let's call her Hannah, who was sexually abused as a child now offers empowering, embodying and healing dance therapy to others.

- A fisherman on Shetland who came to our campervan in one of the times between Covid lockdowns, shouting: 'Do you speak English? Yes? Here's some mackerel for you – just take as many as you'd like! No, no payment needed!'

- And at times it's not even people. There was a street dog in Thailand we named Ridgie. I had slipped and fallen and hurt the top of my feet. Ridgie came to me and very, very gently licked them. She didn't want anything in return – no treats, no scratches. She just felt that I was hurting and gave me comfort.

- The Latvian Lutheran Church, one of the main churches and the biggest Protestant one in the Republic of Latvia, had been ordaining women into ministry since the beginning of the 1970s. 20 years later they were excluded from leadership. Many had to leave their home country. Others struggled to live their calling. In the situation we formed the Association of Women Theologians. Our symbol is a lily breaking though dry, hard ground. There is hope in resilience and strength in perseverance. There is power in resistance!

- A small group of medical students and workers outside the Scottish Parliament, at the Royal Infirmary, at Waverley Station in Edinburgh lighting candles and chanting 'Ceasefire now!' week by week during the bombings of hospitals in Gaza. Students of medicine, medical workers, ordinary people standing in solidarity with medics and patients. Peaceful protest in the face of horrendous violence. Telling the stories of doctors who refused to leave their patients for safety, saying: 'I didn't study medicine to only save my own life, but others.' Saying: 'These people, these patients and medics are my family. I will not leave them.' Speaking the message that people don't seem to learn: that violence isn't a solution. Violence brings suffering and hate and more violence.

At times we do not feel like we are strong and have agency and power, and we need to acknowledge that and use it as best as we can. However, there is also an amazing resilience in us and power to survive, heal and thrive even after the most heart- and bone-breaking events and situations. We just need to reach out – or rather within – for that power and strength – it is there! We need to seek help when that is needed, reach out for human contact, move physically if we can – ideally outside in nature – open up to creativity and spirituality, and we will become resilient.

Blessing

This prayer is for all medical workers in crisis situations but was written for a vigil at the Edinburgh Royal Infirmary for medical workers and patients in Gaza in December 2023. The vigil was organised and led by University of Edinburgh medical students.

Blessed are the medical workers.
Blessed are those who gave their lives
trying to ease the suffering of others.
Blessed are those who gave their lives trying to save other lives.
Blessed are those who didn't leave their patients,
even in the face of danger.
Blessed are those who drove ambulances to save lives in the face of death.
Blessed are those who still operated under attack and amidst rubble.
Blessed are those who offered gentle hands of care
despite violence and destruction.
Blessed are the patients who didn't survive.
Blessed are those who are still surviving.
May all their souls be cradled in God's heart
and on the universe's lap.

Blessed are those who do not give up hope.
Blessed are those who refuse to hate.
Blessed are those who do not kill.
Blessed are those who refuse to separate between 'us and them'.
Blessed are those who give life.
Blessed are those who seek peace rooted in justice.
Blessed are those who care and love to the end.
This is the true power to change the world.
Amen

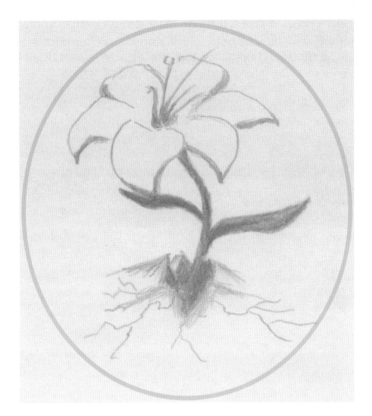

Meditation

Sit comfortably on a chair or a cushion with your back straight and head slightly bent forward. You can close your eyes or just lower your gaze – whatever feels most comfortable to you. Take three deep breaths in and out to let go of some of the tension of the day. Then let your breath return to normal. Spend some time observing your breath. See where you feel it most strongly in your body: is it the movement as the air flows in and out? Or the temperature of the air changing: cooler as you breathe in, warmer as you breathe out? Just observe it. And if something distracts you, a thought, a sound, that's all right. Just turn your attention back to your breath gently and without judgement.

And now I would like to invite you to imagine hard ground – a pavement or concrete. Or dry desert floor, cracked and hard. Imagine it in as much detail as you can: how it looks, the colours, how it would feel beneath your feet or if you touched it with your palm. Maybe imagine how it would smell.

Then imagine a plant breaking through the hard ground.

Imagine the strength and resilience of the plant as it grows tiny bit by bit, pushing against the resistance of the soil or concrete.

Imagine how it comes out into the light and air.

Imagine it spreading its roots and opening its leaves.

Imagine it growing and perhaps forming a flower bud and opening a flower.

Imagine how that might feel.

Now think of a situation where life is hard, where there's injustice, exclusion and oppression and people need to break through like the plant. A situation where resistance and resilience are needed. Then think of how you could support these people. Then go out and do it!

HOLY SATURDAY

Sitting in the dark, waiting for the dawn

Jan Sutch Pickard

Bible readings

After these things, Joseph of Arimathea, who was a disciple of Jesus, though a secret one because of his fear of the Jews, asked Pilate to let him take away the body of Jesus. Pilate gave him permission; so he came and removed his body. Nicodemus, who had at first come to Jesus by night, also came, bringing a mixture of myrrh and aloes, weighing about a hundred pounds. They took the body of Jesus and wrapped it with the spices in linen cloths, according to the burial custom of the Jews. Now there was a garden in the place where he was crucified, and in the garden there was a new tomb in which no one had ever been laid. And so, because it was the Jewish day of Preparation, and the tomb was nearby, they laid Jesus there.

John 19:38–42 (NRSV)

[Joseph] then rolled a great stone to the door of the tomb and went away. Mary Magdalene and the other Mary were there, sitting opposite the tomb.

Matthew 27:60–61 (NRSV)

Reflection

Sitting shiva

The women are *'sitting shiva'*, a silent presence, sharing the absence of one they've loved and lost, accompanying each other in the empty-hands act of mourning.

No other action is possible. On the Sabbath there is nothing else they can do.

Aching, waiting – for what?

They followed the men to the tomb and were there as the battered body of their leader, their son, their friend, was hidden away. There was no time before dusk fell for the women to wash and lay it out – that last careful and loving act. But at least they had his body, were not searching through rubble, were not left unknowing, wildly guessing.

The great stone has been rolled over the mouth of the tomb. It has been sealed. They sit, they wait, and at last they walk home, supporting each other in their grief.

When this long night and day and night are over, some will return, to learn what else they can do. They must not give up. Amid all this conflict and chaos, they will try to sleep, to stay strong. When all hope is gone.

That is the story which we glimpse in fragments from the Gospels: the helpless suffering of Holy Saturday. Jesus cried out on the cross that God had forsaken him, and now it seems he has forsaken those who followed him, believing in a different future. Psalms that the women know by heart rail against human injustice and God's abandonment – but then express hope against hope:

> *Be gracious to me, O Lord. See what I suffer from those who hate me; you are the one who lifts me up from the gates of death. (Psalm 9:13)*

How can that be possible, kneeling amid the rubble of the garden, with memories full of atrocities, in a time of chaos, confronted by death and fear of death and the full-stop of that great rock sealing the tomb?

Leaving space for questions

Each Easter in Iona, when I worked there, we tried to enable the staff team and guests at the Abbey and MacLeod Centre, with folk on the island, to explore the events of Holy Week and Easter 'in real time' – and that still happens. We would walk together from Palm Sunday to Good Friday, using Bible study and creativity of craft and words and symbolic action, pilgrimage, music and liturgy, to tell the story to each other and enter into its meaning for ourselves. A full programme carried strong emotions, needing each of us to be fully focused. After the Stations of the Cross, the Words from the Cross, the stripping of the Abbey Church, when everyone had walked away, alone in the darkness – what then?

Each year, we started to fall into the same trap, of planning programme for Holy Saturday: a choice of workshops … led meditation … a practical activity like planting potatoes … But how can you programme emptiness?

What shape does waiting take – really take – when you don't know what you are waiting for, if there is anything for which to hope?

In Iona we were acting out a story and knew in our hearts where all this was leading. Preparations were well underway for Easter Sunday. The wooden cross we'd carried on Good Friday was secretly being decorated with flowers. Joyful hymns with alleluias were on the service sheet. In the context of a week that explored human and divine suffering and hope, we knew we had come together to celebrate Resurrection.

But in the daily lives we'd come from, and to which we'd be returning – things aren't so predictable. After a death, there's a chaos of emotions: distress, anger, guilt, numbness. We cope by doing things that need to be done, making phone calls, filling forms, sorting belongings, planning for a funeral. We try to create some kind of order, where there is none. Our faith falters. We may call it a waiting time – but what are we waiting for?

In the Land called Holy the climate and the culture mean that funerals should happen very soon after death. In a time of war, that may not happen, making the distress even greater. If the body can't be identified, or is buried under rubble: where's your Holy Saturday then?

Another story

The early Church held on to a tradition which was a radically different way of coping. It's a story not found in any of the four Gospels but in the apocryphal Gospel of Nicodemus. We're reminded of it when we affirm our faith:

> *A man of compassion, he died forsaken,*
> *he descended into the earth, to the place of death.*
> *On the third day he rose from the tomb …*[1]

These words are from the *Iona Abbey Worship Book*. Some of us may be more familiar with 'He descended into hell.' Those words evoke not the passive stillness of the body in the rock-hewn tomb, but something else. Not the slipping away into Sheol of Jewish belief: for early Christians what happened between Christ's crucifixion and resurrection took on a more dynamic meaning. I'm not a student of the Gospel of Nicodemus, but in religious art from many cultures, and mediaeval texts like Langland's *Piers Plowman* and the Mystery plays, I've glimpsed this other story. It's one of heroic, cosmic action: the Harrowing of Hell.

In the Middle Ages craft guilds took the story of Salvation, starting from Creation, onto the streets in promenade performances. Revivals give a sense of an energetic, literal approach to faith: possibly heretical, also poetical and humorous. The Harrowing of Hell would have featured a gaping monstrous Hell's Mouth, behind which a crowd of lost souls huddled – Adam and Eve, the prophets, and ordinary men and women, including the repentant thief, all waiting for a redeemer. In one text Isaiah says:

> *The people ... that went about in thesterness (darkness)*
> *see a full great lightness, as we do now, each one.*

Satan and a gang of demons, who were gloating over their captives, begin to be afraid. Then comes the loud climax – a stage direction from the *Chester Pageant of the Cooks and Innkeepers* includes all their pots and pans as well as words from Psalm 24:

> *Then shall come Jesus, and a clamour shall be made, or a loud sound of*
> *things striking together, and let Jesus say: 'Lift up your heads, O ye*
> *gates; and be ye lift up, ye everlasting doors; and the King of Glory shall*
> *come in.* [2]

Jesus leads the ransomed souls out through Hell's Mouth. Soon the stone will be rolled away from the tomb. This drama, this communal clamour of victory, could be a way of coping with the hopelessness of Holy Saturday.

But I know that today that many people are still in a hell of humanity's making. What can I do? Where is God in all this? Who will roll away the stone? We are just sitting in the dark, waiting for the dawn.

Prayer for Holy Saturday

Sit down here with us, God,
in our helplessness, grieving
for a broken world:
we believe that you, too,
deeply grieve.

Wait with us, God,
even when we don't know
why we are waiting –
how long it will be –
for your patience is eternal.

Encourage us, God,
amid chaos, clamour of conflict:
thesterness, smoke hiding the sky:
you know our distress
at so much suffering.
When it is very dark,
give hope that dawn will come.
Amen

Some questions to think about

In the description of the burial of Jesus, do you think we need both Matthew's account and John's? Why?

Which of the three sections in the reflection: the description of the mourning women, the Iona dilemma, the dramatisation of the Harrowing of Hell, comes alive for you?

Is there value in learning a 'new' word (*thesterness*) for darkness? As you will have realised, the context of this reflection and prayer is the carnage in Gaza, Israel, the West Bank, as I write. Have there been any points in the last year when you have been lost for words, when the news has been 'beyond words dreadful'? How do you cope with that?

Notes:

1. From *Iona Abbey Worship Book,* Wild Goose Publications, 2001

2. From the Chester Mystery Plays, circa 1540

Easter Sunday

There is hope

Stef Benstead, Church Action on Poverty

Bible readings

On this mountain the Lord of hosts will make for all peoples
   a feast of rich food, a feast of well-aged wines,
   of rich food filled with marrow, of well-aged wines strained clear.
And he will destroy on this mountain
   the shroud that is cast over all peoples,
   the covering that is spread over all nations;
   he will swallow up death forever.
Then the Lord God will wipe away the tears from all faces,
   and the disgrace of his people he will take away from all the earth,
   for the Lord has spoken.
It will be said on that day,
   'See, this is our God; we have waited for him, so that he might save us.
   This is the Lord for whom we have waited;
   let us be glad and rejoice in his salvation.'

Isaiah 25:6–9 (NRSV)

Then Peter began to speak to them: 'I truly understand that God shows no par-
tiality, but in every people anyone who fears him and practises righteousness is
acceptable to him. You know the message he sent to the people of Israel,
preaching peace by Jesus Christ – he is Lord of all. That message spread
throughout Judea, beginning in Galilee after the baptism that John announced:
how God anointed Jesus of Nazareth with the Holy Spirit and with power; how
he went about doing good and healing all who were oppressed by the devil, for
God was with him.'

Acts 10:34–38 (NRSV)

Reflection

As someone living with chronic illness, it feels like a lot of my life is spent
waiting. Waiting for the day to end so I can go back to bed. Waiting to see if
a new course of treatment will make any difference. Waiting for my sister's
kids to be a bit older so my (also ill) sister no longer needs as much help from
me. Waiting for appointments. Waiting for results from appointments.
Waiting for the pain to stop. Waiting for energy to return.

But by far the biggest thing I find myself waiting and longing for is heaven. Chronic illness is like living in a perpetual Easter Saturday: Jesus has died, and with him the lifeblood of your party. All your hopes, dreams and plans for the future are gone, never to return. There is no recovery from chronic illness; no escape from the daily pain and exhaustion; no escape from the fact that everything you do is hard.

Over the course of Maundy Thursday and Good Friday the disciples had watched the slow crushing of all their hopes and everything they believed in. Now, on Easter Saturday, they were left with completely nothing. They had no idea that this was not to be their permanent state.

Perhaps they remembered Job's cry 'I know that my redeemer lives'. Perhaps they recalled Jesus' words about seeds falling to the ground and dying. Perhaps they were too overwhelmed with grief and dismay to think of anything at all.

But as Christians, we never live through Easter Saturday. Whatever the travails we experience on earth, we live through them in the sure and certain knowledge of the hope of the new heaven and earth. We live through difficulties knowing that they are nothing but the valley of the shadow of death; the shadow of a defeated enemy who cannot keep us from the table set for us with its overflowing cup. We know that all the sufferings and frustrations of this earth will one day be completely removed. We are promised that we may enjoy this new heaven and earth with God forever.

This promise is for any person who fears God and does what is right. It is for everyone who believes in Jesus and thereby receives forgiveness of sins through His name.

This belief in Jesus is not a passive thing; a mere intellectual acknowledgement that God exists and that the only way to him is through Jesus. It is possible to acknowledge the truth of these statements and choose to live in rebellion with God. The demons do it all the time. Rather, to believe in God is to make a decision to stop living in rebellion to him and to start living in obedience and relationship. It means an earnest desire to know God's will in order to obey it; a longing to bring glory and honour to God through the way we live.

Living in Easter Sunday as we do, we understand that our justification before God is by faith in Jesus' death for us. We also understand that faith is an active thing which we live day by day, seeking to honour and obey our God. Jesus himself 'went about doing good and healing/saving all those oppressed by the devil'. Luke, the author of Acts, uses his gospel to portray salvation as a multifaceted thing: not just spiritual and for the future, but also physical, relational and for the present. Jesus came to heal all disease, end all demonic oppression, restore broken relationships and renew all things. He started this with his ministry on earth; he continues it today; and he will complete it on his second coming.

If the only thing that mattered about salvation was going to heaven when we die, then the years that Jesus spent in active ministry wouldn't have mattered much. The gospel writers needn't have bothered recording them for us. Once Jesus had antagonised the authorities into wanting him dead, the Bible could have skipped straight to the crucifixion. Instead, the physical reality that Jesus brought is also important. God wanted, and wants, to reduce suffering in this in-between time.

The completeness of Jesus' salvation offers me huge hope. There is hope because broken relationships will be healed. There is hope for those who are the least and the poorest in society, because poverty and oppression will not exist. There is hope because the pain that I live with every day will be completely gone.

The fact that this physical reality matters to God right now is a comfort to me. Even if I never experience healing this side of eternity, nevertheless I know that we have a God to whom it matters that I am suffering. I hold on to that in the light of Easter Sunday as I look forward to Jesus' second coming.

Prayer

Thank you, God, for your death, resurrection and ascension as Jesus. Thank you for your overwhelming love, which sent you to come and seek and save the lost, even when we were very far from you. Thank you for your concern for us here on earth now, as well as your concern for our future dwelling with you in the new heaven and earth.

Inspire us through your love to love and worship you. May we so understand the extent of your grace that we find it naturally pouring out of us to others. May we long and strive to show your love to others, so that we, your body, may be your hands and feet in this world.

Encourage us in our difficulties to fix our eyes on you and wait patiently for your second coming and the new heaven and earth. Thank you for the blessing of Easter Sunday, which gives us hope no matter what our circumstances. Amen

Meditation

Imagine it is Easter Saturday. You had been following a man whom you thought was God incarnate, who would lead your people out of economic servitude to the Romans and out of spiritual servitude to the Pharisees. You thought he had the words of life. You had lived closely with him for three years as his friends as well as his disciples. You loved him and looked up to him.

But now he is dead. How do you feel? Think about how other grief has made you feel, and how that might compare to what the disciples felt at losing not just a friend but their Saviour.

Now it is Easter Sunday. First the women tell you that the tomb is empty; then one of them says she has seen Jesus. Later, two other disciples of Jesus tell you that they met him on the road to Emmaus. Finally, you see him yourself. Your God is so great that even death cannot defeat him!

What hope is inspired in you by the resurrection of Jesus? What confidence does this give you in God and his salvation? Hold on to this as you live through trials on this earth, waiting for the full coming of Jesus.

Easter Monday

To set all people free

Alex and Jo Clare-Young

Bible readings

And God said, 'Let there be lights in the vault of the sky to separate the day from the night, and let them serve as signs to mark sacred times, and days and years …' And God saw that it was good.

Genesis 1:14,18b (NRSV)

It is sown a physical body, it is raised a spiritual body. If there is a physical body, there is also a spiritual body. Thus it is written, 'The first man, Adam, became a living being'; the last Adam became a life-giving spirit. But it is not the spiritual that is first, but the physical, and then the spiritual. The first man was from the earth, a man of dust; the second man is from heaven. As was the man of dust, so are those who are of the dust; and as is the man of heaven, so are those who are of heaven. Just as we have borne the image of the man of dust, we will also bear the image of the man of heaven.

1 Corinthians 44–49 (NRSV)

Reflection

The writer of the Genesis creation myths recognised that there are sacred times – hours, days and years – that humans need to mark in particular ways, to notice the spark of God's energy within themselves and around them in the world. It is fitting, then, that at this time of year, just after Easter, that the lectionary takes us to Genesis and to Paul's first letter to the Corinthians to ponder the origins of human beings and of the world in which we live.

Paul's words need to be read with care, though, and with an attentiveness to the words in Genesis that he is paraphrasing here. The 'first man' that Paul refers to is described in the first chapter of Genesis as *ha'adam* – the human, or humankind. *Adam* here is not a male name but, rather, points to the earth-iness of humankind, to our origins in the ruddy clay of earth, the temporal dust of stars, the tentative joining of atoms.

More than the physical, though, *ha'adam* points to the relational realities of being human. And no, I do not mean the binary juxtapositions that lead to heterosexism/cissexism. Rather I am pointing to the dialogical dance of being human. Genesis describes humanity as diverse and at the centre of its mythological message is a pertinent reminder that humans are at our best when we are in genuine dialogue and creative endeavour between ourselves and those who are both alike and different from us, and between ourselves and God.

Paul picks up yet another thread within the Genesis tapestry – the fleshiness and the holiness of human beings. For Paul, our being enfleshed and our being in God are both important but, he suggests, in Christ God is doing something new. In this new, post-resurrection world, we are freed from the limits of being a body into the potential of being the body. In contemporary English, Paul's description of what it is to be human might read something like this:

> *'You are made of stardust and soil, of imagination and identity. Yes, the body came first, but you are both body and spirit. God keeps doing a new thing.'*

So what does this angle on what it means to be human lend us today, as we look back on Easter, and forward towards Pentecost? It seems to me that we live in an increasingly bleak and divided world, where seeing is believing, being right is held as more important than being kind, and religious institutions are more likely to insist on normative patterns of living according to bodily and societal norms than to encourage their members, and society more widely, to dare to live out into new, creative dreams. Paul paints an enticing picture of an alternative reality, a subculture in which we might recognise that life is more than it seems, a movement in which we might together embody something of God.

Easter, and later Pentecost, are each a clear nexus of change. This is not a limiting, trapping, depressing change. No, at Easter, and then at Pentecost, there is a kind of liberationist revolution in some people's understandings of God and the limits that God placed on humankind.

The events of Easter seem to be sparked by the idea, held by an occupying army, that Jesus is somehow dangerous – in today's language, he might be seen as woke, socialist or perhaps even a radical. And then God seemingly breaks the bounds of human fleshiness, enabling Jesus to appear to those who loved and were challenged by him in recognisable words and actions – in dialogue. Later, at Pentecost, the limits of the body are transcended once more as those disciples become agents of change through their adoption into the body of Christ – a body that is inevitably queer, trans, disabled, neurodiverse and many hues. A body that defies limiting expectations or death-oriented binarism and debates.

So, this Easter Monday, I wonder what it might feel like to transcend our own expectations – the ones that trap ourselves, and those that – in our minds and sometimes in our words and actions – trap others. I wonder what it might be like to dare to actively image the God who breaks through, who breaks out, and who sets all people free. I wonder what it might be like to engage in the dialogical work of being the body of Christ – diverse, messy, creative, and full of potential. But to do that we must break down our boxes and stretch beyond our definitions and debates. We must stop pointing at 'them' and start embracing 'us'. We must stop living as if we, as individuals, have what everyone else needs and start to live as if we need each other.

We are at a nexus, a turning point, a crossroad. Where shall we travel next? Who shall we travel with? How will we join in God's creative endeavour to set all people free?

Prayer

Here we are, God,
people of soil and stardust,
people of body and spirit,
people of stillness and dance.

Here we are, God,
diverse, creative, confused, enfleshed and holy.

Here we are, God,
ready for you to do something new with us.
Trying to see the invisible threads that can mend a divided world.
Trying to see the 'us' in them.
And more importantly the 'them' in us.

Meditation

Look around you: who are your travelling companions? Look for those pil-grims on the road with you that perhaps you have not noticed before, whose voices you might lift up, and whose spirits might lift you up.

How can you join in God's creative endeavour to set all people free?

Are you just listening? Just speaking? Or in dialogue … with God? With others? With yourself?

As you dance towards marking the sacred time of Pentecost – will you try a new step?

RESOURCES

POEMS AND PRAYERS

THE ROAD TO THE CROSS

These eight poems, contemplating the road to the Cross, draw on traditional legend and scriptural narrative.

Stations of the Cross

These stations are places
Where we pause and gaze, fixed
In a timeless moment
Of devotion. Linking us with countless thousands
Of worshippers, now and ages past.
A place of standing, watchfulness
And waiting, where we trace
In frail imagination the slow steps
Of Christ from condemnation to the cross.
Here legend and scripture meet and mingle.
Just as truth, distilled in the imagination,
Can tell us so much more than factual narrative,
Story holds truths that infiltrate our minds and change us
Because they touch the core of us, the nerve, raw and alert.

But these are our stations, utterly different, holding memory:
Places of waiting on sweeping platforms,
Arrival and departure,
Separation and expectation,
Loss and greeting.
But these were not stations for him,
No pausing on this journey, the waiting is over,
The separations, the departing friends, fled.
Now, flanked by legionaries eager
To get the brutal job done, shoving
The crowd aside, merciless to force him forward.
Simon, press-ganged to carry the cross beam,
Forced to keep the pace through streets full of eyes,
Of mouths, gaping grotesque in horror or sly anticipation
Of such public pain.
And legend tells us that he stumbled, fell,
And Gospel, that he spoke.

What instinctive truth
Waits for us here, at each station of this journey?

Thorns

The show trial limped wearily through the night.
False witnesses, stumbling over one another
To earn their fee. The soldiers bored and restless,
Religious and politicians smug in their expediency,
Shrugging off the horror
Of their judgement. A temporary alliance.
The gaping crowd now drifts away
To wineshop, gossip, darkened streets
And the huge indifference of other lives.

He is alone, despite encircling faces:
Moments of waiting
Before the torment begins, and then it breaks on him.
The mockery of kingship, the robe and reed, the agony of flogging.
And one man, young perhaps,
Desperate to prove himself a man,
Not old enough to know the endurance of pain
Only the casual cruelties that make your fellows laugh;
One man rips a bush out of the ground,
Twisting thorns, thick as thumbs, into a crown.
Laughing, the company of them, bored,
Half-dreading the brutality of their duty,
Laughing, they thrust the circlet onto his head,
Watching the blood spurt out and trickle thickly down his face.

What crown was given him?
The kingdoms of this world,
The costly weight of government,
The tyrannies and abuse of power.
Kingdoms held together by oppression
Or dismembered by greed.
All earthly power was crushed upon his head
With all its pain and sorrow.
And from his cross he saw and bore the slow millennia

Turning. Empires rising and falling, conquest
And dominion.
It was Adam's curse that crushed him,
Thorns and servitude, hard labour,
Serfdom, slavery, gathered into a mockery of a crown,
Yet borne with patient and unfailing hope.

Jesus falls the first time

Stones, more brutal than a boxer's knuckles
Rose up to smash and graze his knees,
His battered feet.
Did he hear, in that moment of falling,
Ironic laughter, echoing down the years of ministry,
'Lest you dash your foot against a stone'?
Falling, with all the haplessness of childhood,
Falling beneath the heavy cross beam
That jarred and crushed his shoulder and his neck.
Outspread hands, that could not save him
From his fall, our fall, the desperate vulnerability
Of his fully owned humanity.
Not all the legions of angels, nor
His own divinity
Could spare him this, his choice
To enter fully into our fragile nature
And say, 'This is my body'. This flesh
Of bone and nerve, of pain and nakedness,
Of blood, tears and sweat, thirst and hunger,
And now of weary agony,
This body, enduring all, incorporating all
Into himself.

There were no angels here to bear him up,
Just the rough wrenching of a legionnaire's grip
To set him on his feet again, and smite him forwards.

Jesus sees his mother

She, held roughly back by soldiers guarding the route,
He, stumbling forward,
Blind with acid sweat and blood,
Their eyes meeting, no touch, no embrace,
No words. They would come later.
All the love and the shared pain, of more than thirty years,
Leaping between them in that meeting.
Did she remember then,
The sword that would pierce her heart
Spoken of so long ago
And wrenched within her so terribly now?
She knew this destiny he had chosen to fulfil,
Had glimpsed it often, even in his childhood,
Remembering her own calling to give him birth
And the cost of that, stigma and terror,
The sharp straw on which she laid him,
The weary churning dust of the roads,
Asylum seeker in Egypt. And the fear of Herod.

She knew his power to change the water into wine,
Even then recognising
That this was no easy miracle
But would one day be fulfilled at the cost of his own blood
To make the wine of life.
She knew too, a carpenter's wife,
The exact nature of his dying
Against the splintered wood,
And the nails, wedges of rough iron,
And the heavy mallets that would drive them home.

Who knows his thoughts?
His pity and compassion for her
Standing so bravely alone
To watch his journey and be with him at its close,
Even as she had been with him at its earthly beginning.
His gratitude that, even to that dreadful end,
Despite all bewilderment and deep distress,

She had not swerved away from serving him,
Loving him, and even now, if she could enfold him
In the safety of her own body she would do so,
And yet, knowing as she did what was the greater love,
Releasing him,
That all things might be made new.

Veronica wipes the face of Jesus

Mark her, as she thrusts forward,
Her hands stretched out, the cloth, wet with tears
As well as water,
The soldiers, touched perhaps with sudden pity,
Letting her slip between them,
To see her take such simple love,
Such a simple gift, a moment's refreshment,
To wipe away the terrible travail of his journey.
Who knows the truth of the legend? Yet
All would wish they could have found such courage
To press forward and be a part
Of this most agonised of roads. She, bearing the image
Wiped from his face in sweat and blood,
Holding in her heart the face, familiar then
But unseen now, and showing us how tenderness
Reveals his countenance in acts of kindness,
Captured in those lineaments of grace.
Revealing to us how the suffering Christ is seen
In all the faces of the destitute and tormented,
The abused, the persecuted and the refugee,
The crushed and rejected
That are the true ikon of his likeness.

Jesus meets the grieving women of Jerusalem

If we had ears to hear, we might have heard
The stones cry out. Not in worship
But in horror that such suffering should stumble
Over them. Such cruelty, such ruthlessness,
Here in Zion, the beloved city.
But the ancient stones are mute,
And the crowd, fenced in by soldiery,
Has fallen silent now. The mob, hired
To jeer for his crucifixion, has slunk away,
Their voices shamed to silence.
The disciples, too, in agony of thought,
Have hidden away, their world undone.

But there, linked by love and a defiant courage,
The women force their way past an unnerved soldiery,
Women who had followed him from Galilee,
Women who have gathered from the courtyards and streets
Of Jerusalem, melded in their shared distress,
Their tormented hands, moving in ancient ritualised gestures,
Their tears, flowing as though deep had called to deep
To release the hidden springs.
And now he sees them, pauses, turns,
Straightening the torn back,
Looking through bruised and blurred eyes
To see these clustered, despairing women
And take their pain into himself.
As he does so, it seems as if the world stops,
Guttural commands fall silent, the murmur of the crowd
Dies away, and there is only their terrible grief
And his voice.
Do not weep for me. Do not weep for me.
It is yourselves and your children who will bear
This unspeakable cost. You will say then that women
Are blessed who have not borne children,
Who do not fear the terrible vulnerability
Of women and their babies

Under siege.
I would have offered sanctuary, O Jerusalem,
But you could not recognise me.
And now weep, not only for yourselves,
But for all those in the centuries to come
Who will be helpless in the cruel hands and ambitions
Of warlords, of besieging princes who hate peace
And lust for power.
The countless women and children, who become
The spoils of war.
Weep for them.
And he saw the dreadful unravelling
Of kindness at the heart of history.

Weep, women of Jerusalem, weep
For Palestine and her mothers,
For Yemen's children, for the slaughtered women
Of Bosnia, for girls stolen in Nigeria,
Raped in the Republic of the Congo,
For child soldiers, deceived into cruelty,
For young women trafficked into Britain,
For women and girls in Afghanistan
And Sudan.
Weep not for me, he said, knowing
All the anguish that lay ahead, yet the hope of resurrection,
Which in its time will make all things new
And heal the tears of the world.
Weep not for me, but add your tears to the balm
That will bring justice to the oppressed,
Restore the kinship of humanity,
And consolation
To the broken minds and bodies
Wrecked and racked by time.

If we have ears to hear,
The stones, aghast, are weeping now,
Crushed beneath the indifferent feet
Of generations.

Stripped of his garments

As he was born into the world,
Naked except for blood and the waters of birth,
So now they stripped him,
Drawing on that age-old sense of shame,
That vulnerability and exposure.
And while they gambled for his garments
Did they pause to contemplate
That seamless robe and wonder
At the love and skill that would have made it for him
At the terrible contrast of his helplessness
And the devotion that it showed?
And as they diced for his death
Did they hear the words of forgiveness?
That extraordinary gift releasing them, and everyone
Involved in the trial and the horror of it,
From the dread and blame of generations
Who would demand wrath and persecution
As though they held a mandate
For the judgement of God.

And now exposed, most fully revealing
The incarnate presence of God,
The flesh in which he had glorified God
Full of grace and truth.
Now, for those who could see,
God was naked before them,
At one with all the generations of humiliation,
The shame of the woman dragged before him in the Temple court,
The thousands of his fellow Jews
Naked before their murderers at Babi Yar.

Most truly one with us,
Love and mercy, words of grace and healing,
Revealed in the extremity of his pinioned limbs,
His battered, weary body.
Was it this that caused the officer to exclaim
'Truly this man was a son of God.'

Words

His mother stood watching with the other women,
Throughout the aching hours of that day,
But she alone could remember
The tearing agony of his birth,
His first cry,
The cloths with which she wound him.
Just as now they had brought cloths
To enfold his body after death
And give him rest.
Perhaps she remembered that cry as she heard him
Cry out that all was completed now, both
Coming from that searing place in the lungs,
The first from the abandoning of the womb
The gasp of air, and now this the great conclusion of his life,
The entry into the eternal, the preface to the return
To his Father.
She might have heard it as a cry whose ripples would spread out
As those stirred by a pebble tossed into the water,
Spreading out and out beyond sight,
Disturbing currents in the depths,
And now travelling out beyond hearing
To fill and resonate the furthest corners
Of the universe.

She would have heard all words
Spoken from the pinnacle of the cross and seen their meaning,
Their coherence. The forgiveness; the promise of Paradise;
The thirst (poignant reminder of his infant dependence on her);
The agony of the cry of abandonment,
That most human cry of alienation and distress
When even Fatherhood seems silent.
But before that, those moments of intimacy
And provision.

John had somehow dared to return
And stood beside her, watching with her,
And it was to them Jesus spoke: your son, your mother,
That neither should be alone to carry the burden of grief
Or fear the future. And in so doing
He spoke prophetically of a renewed community,
An uncomplicated priority
Of love and relationship across generations,
Across gender and age and all diversity, the epitome
Of what should be called church.
She heard his words, and now within the sheltering arm
Of John, his words and even the slow
Agonising process of her Son's death became bearable.
She remembered other words, 'My time has not yet come',
And knew their meaning. And then
After he surrendered his spirit, she saw the water and the blood
Pour from his side, and all things became one:
His birth, his death. She remembered angels
And shepherds, and the strange wise men coming from the East,
And the flight to Egypt.
And now this: soon, soon, they would take him down
From the cross, wrenching out the nails and wrapping him
With tenderness, and laying him in a tomb.
Beyond that she was not sure, but she knew
It would be wonderful.
Weeping now, enduring for a night of bewildering
And devastating loss,
But, mysteriously, not without hope
That radiant joy would come in the morning.

Janet Killeen

A prayer for Ukraine

For the yellow and blue nation –
the yellow land of wheat and sunflowers,
the blue sky of hope and peace:

may bullies not prosper,
may those who make war,
draw back,
may those who terrorise others,
understand kindness.

Holy Creator, God of icons and incense,
Refugee Christ, inhabiting an occupied land,
Hopeful Spirit of truth and reconciliation,

may you, the eternal Three-in-One,
dance in the fields and skies of Ukraine,
binding up the wounded,
embracing the fearful,
ushering in a life of peace with justice.

May we who, from afar,
see the terrors, injury and damage,
stand alongside all those who
genuinely seek peace.

Janet Lees

Sleepless

Tonight, back home,
I've found the safe space of my own bed,
and coorie down, because the house is cold;
across the dark familiar street,
I hear the sea breathe in its sleep.

Cradled here, I find my mind
can't rest: descends long stairs

into a subway, explores
strange halls and corridors,
and takes a last flight deeper still

in company of human beings
in hundreds, each with a face,
huddled families, cuddled children
bundled against the chill,
sitting in silence on the steps
unsleeping, underground

listening – from this fragile shelter –
as terror starts to possess
a once-familiar place:
facts on the ground
like waves breaking over our heads.

Jan Sutch Pickard

Through the wood: Remembering Jesus' last sayings from the Cross

You'll need a big enough cross for the centre of the space. It could be wood, paper, card or chalked on the floor.

You'll also need some pieces of paper and pencils for people to write their remembered 'Last words from the Cross' on, and a means to fix these to the cross. This will depend on what the cross is made of: use pins, or some sort of adhesive, or just sticky notes.

Begin with the sounds of a jeering crowd and shouts of 'Crucify!' from a recording, or random sounds of the same from the people gathered together.

Prayer:

When a tree was planted,
no one knew what it would become.

When a tree was growing,
no one knew its destiny.

When a tree was felled,
no one knew how it would be used.

Silence

Invite people to approach the cross and leave their remembered version of any of Jesus' last words there. They may choose to speak them aloud as they place them on the cross, or not, as they prefer.

Closing prayer:

Christ of the cross, as you hung on for us,
may we hang on with and for each other,
and be mindful of our calling to be your body.

Reconciling One, from sapling to servant, you call us.
Bring us back into balance:
may we know the Earth as our one precious home.
Through the wood you call us
and by our prayers we touch you again.
Form us into your likeness:
make us your body, through the wood.

Janet Lees, Lay Community of St Benedict

Iona: Storm imminent

The wind rises,
the waves roll in,
no ferry dares to show its face
and the nights are drawing in;
yet carried on a quickening breeze is
Cassandra calling:
'Beware the tides of March.'

Still migrant birds come flying by,
pause their passage,
partake of food
and rest their weary wings
before moving on to gentler climes.

So, for a time,
the curlew's mournful cries
haunt our skies
and greylag geese, en masse,
descend to strip our fields until,
disturbed, derange the whole isle
with their honking spiel
so drown the sound of
Cassandra calling:
'Beware the tides of March.'

And autumn's penetrating light
captures contours,
paints vibrant colours
to show the landscape's
every form and palette
and so reveal the stark nature
of primeval forces gathering,
triggered by our dithering,
our failure to compensate
the plunder of our planet.

So with cloth ears and airbrushed lives,
tick-tock, tick-tock, time is running out
as our petty pleasures we consume
so we ourselves shall be consumed
baked by the sun
on earth eaten by the ocean
and reap our thoughtlessness
when we disregard
Cassandra calling:
'Beware the tides of March.'

The wind rises,
the waves roll in,
caring nothing of what we say or do,
they froth, foam and break
across the pier washing down the street,

a taste of things to come,
and on these waves comes surfing in
Cassandra calling:
'Beware the tides of March.'

Mark Scholefield, 2022

ECO-PSALMS FROM IONA

Many today feel that the Earth itself, and the body of all creation, is being cruci-fied. They hear the cry of creation and want to live differently. These eco-psalms were written by guests at Iona Abbey in 2022. Thanks to Patrick Small, Abbey Programme Worker, for sending me these. (Ed.)

All creation sings your praise

We thank you God for:
all the colours of nature around us.
The contrasts of the countryside in green, white and pink.
The beautiful blue of skies and sea and lips after swimming.
The feeling of cold, of clear water, and the colours of the seaweed.
The greens of grass and bracken in its fractal beauty,
even in the rain.
Of moss on rocks in all its colours.
The colours of the plants and flowers – for purple!
For the views from the top of hills and everything we see.
For perspective and clarity, for the sunshine after rain.
For the wind that gives us power.
For the power of the waves and the rising tide around the islands.
For all the animals and birds, mink and sheep.
Puffins, penguins and oyster-catchers sitting proudly on the rocks.
For the voices of happy humans and friends
who wave to us across the waves.
For hot showers and hot cocoa at the end of the day.

All creation sings your praise.
We thank you for the wonders you have made.
Amen

By the youth of Westminster Presbyterian Church, Austin, Texas

Your hurting, crying world

Rock of ages …
mined, blasted, crushed, formed into yet more stuff.

All things praise thee …
But no one hears the voices of the great auk, the dodo,
the Tasmanian wolf.

Who is on the Lord's side? …
Not the corporations of this world,
nor many of the political establishment.

What a friend we have in Jesus …
Yet who will be a friend to the poor, the oppressed, the hungry,
the non-human world?

May the mind of Christ my Saviour …
whatsoever things are true … think on these things.

Love divine, all loves excelling …
melt my heart of stone,
revive my compassion for your hurting,
crying world.

Go forth and tell …
Equip me, Lord, to be part of the solution.

Euan McPhee

For generations to come

O God, why is the world such a mess?
Why will people not listen?
We are greedy and we have allowed this to influence
how we use our resources.
Let us stand back and look at what has happened.

When the world stopped for COVID things started to regenerate.
The air became cleaner
flowers bloomed

insects increased
bees hummed
birds sang …

We must not go back to the old ways.
We must look forward and take care of our Earth
for the sake of generations to come.

Christine Rowntree

Do we not hear?

Corncrake and skylark,
oystercatcher and fulmar
cry plaintively on the wind.

Scottish heather orchid,
buttercup, daisy, and wild thyme
beseech as well;
these, softly,
so softly,
so very softly,
do these flowers speak,
that you and I must
fall to our knees,
draw close,
so close,
as we might
were we to wash their feet;
that we might hear,
hear fully,
the whispers of their
suffering song.

Foamy seas murmur along the
far machair,
sand and cobble strand marking
the very edge of the world,
bearing the call and cry

of every wave
of all the world's seas,
wind-driven,
wind-borne.

You and I,
do we not hear?
Do we not hear?
Do we not hear the voice
of Creation calling –
nay, sobbing,
weeping?

Weeping borne on the wind,
each bird,
flower,
wave of the broad seas:
a voice,
each in its own way,
and as a gathered
single voice,
the voice of
Rachel weeping.

Rachel weeping for
her children –
   Earth
      Water
         Air.
She calls in her
anguished weeping
to you
and to me.

Oh, my children!
Save,
oh save these,
my children –
   Earth

Water
        Air.
She weeps!
Save these!
These are my children!

You and I,
do we not hear her weeping?
You, and I,
do we not hear?

Doug Dunlap

In our times of anger

God, we are so angry. We are not angry with you, but with those you love who ignore what we believe is how you want us all to live. We are angry with the polluters; the greedy corporations who seem to control our lives; the politicians who sell us falsehoods and do not confront us with the issues that really need sorting; those who do not see or care about the connections between all the different parts of your world.

Despite this, we try to temper our anger and despair by acknowledging and rejoicing in those who value biodiversity; who develop alternative sources of energy; who see the value of the local; who try to educate others; and who stand up for Kingdom values.

In our times of anger, of despair at the lack of positive change, and at our inability to make a difference, help us to be consoled and strengthened by the good and valuable things that are being done in your name, so that we may carry these with us in hope and that hope may lead us to action for the common good.

Simon Rowntree

Where are you, God?

Where are you, God, when we destroy your creation?
Where are you when we turn a blind eye?
Where are you, God, when we strive only for profit?
Where are you when we stray down this path?

When we call to you will you answer?
Will you lend us your righteous anger?
When we cry to you will you wipe our tears
and turn them into rivers of justice?

You are there, God, when we replant your trees.
You are there when we march in the streets.
You are there, God, when we find new solutions.
You are there to guide us back to this path.

Catriona Gorton

You are with us

Lord, we have done so much damage to your creation,
your beautiful gift to us.
We see the effects of consumerism, corporate power and geopolitics
which do not value the earth.
Through industry, pollution, poverty and war,
we deny you and your bounty, provided for all.

Yet you are with us, and support us in our efforts to change.
You inspire your people, young and old, to work for the environment.
We plant trees and flowers, use renewable energy and build sustainably.
We shop local, work from home, cycle and use public transport.
And we show others a new way of living, as stewards of your creation.
We share resources and ideas, making change possible for all.
Lord, you call us on to do more, go further, bring others with us.
And you bless us in our work.

Fiona Gorton

God of relationship

Where can I go? What can I do? How do I become a gardener in your creation, Lord? I don't know where to start, how to make an impact, when every action has a reaction. In a global economy where food comes from around the world – sometimes from places of want where goods are manufactured in harmful ways to both people and the environment, to places of riches. What do I do, how do I demonstrate love for your world? How do I show love to my community and love across the world? It all seems so immense, what difference do I make? I can't fix it all, I can't even take it all in. I can become overwhelmed by it all.

Then I come back to you. What did you do? I look to the life of Christ – his ministry to the individual. I can reach out on the small scale – every small action has an impact, even the tiny pebbles make ripples in a pond. You are the God of the individual, my God, so my actions and reactions matter. You are also the God of love who, as a loving parent, understands when I, your child, struggle, fail, resist, downright disobey and yet you love me unfailingly still. In the face of that what can I do? It all comes down to relationship with God the parent, Christ the brother, Spirit the light within. Relationship with community – family – friends – church – work colleagues – the local community and the wider world. Right relationship builds and nurtures, wrong relationship, self-seeking relationship, destroys. God of relationship, help me have and sustain good relationships.

Paula Callam

The Earth was the Lord's

The Earth was the Lord's – and everything in it!
Then humankind was created
and the Earth was put in their hands.
Wars came.
Pollution was caused.
Species were driven to extinction.
The temperature rose.
The seas rose.
The land ceased to produce.

The humans died.
Then the Earth was the Lord's again and everything in it!

Martin Callam

Continuously creative

Creator God,
      passionate lover of all you create,
      you are continuously   creative
                              inspiring
                              transforming
                              renewing
                              life-giving
re-birthing
restoring
never-ending
never-tiring
never hopeless.

But I am weary. I feel helpless.

The mountains of disposed plastic
                    wasted food
                    discarded remains
I see every day overwhelm me.
So much spillage and destruction of your planet and its people
that is beyond my control.

But you designed life to be sustained by love
for all you create.

Our interdependence is of you, embedded in creation itself.
So despite all circumstances that overwhelm, deny, stifle,
pollute and destroy,
I will determine to trust you, to listen,
to pray, to speak out,
to live and work for your purpose
all my days.

For you are … continuously creative …

By an Abbey guest

Sing a new song

All: Sing a new song, all the earth.
         Sing a new song to God.
A: Call out consumerism!
         Crush corporate power!
All: Sing a new song to God.

B: Put public transport before cars!
         Press for alternative energy sources!
All: Sing a new song to God.

A: Resource low-tech solutions!
         Rewild the land!
All: Sing a new song to God.

B: Love localism!
         Legislate for the earth!
All: Sing a new song, all the earth.
         Sing a new song to God.

Margaret Crawshaw

After Thomas (A Camas poem)

I believe in the lark
although I cannot see it
against the sun –
suddenly so much April light
suffusing the moor,
where peat-cuttings
and muirburn black
remember winter's long night;

now, a new beginning –
with this small bird
such a vital part,
overflowing the morning
with what feels like joy;
I paused on the worn track
where the sound struck a spark –
now the long song
goes on, far beyond me,
shimmering out of sight;

beyond doubt, the lark
can be at once
sky-high and down-to-earth,
heard but not seen;
we need no written evidence,
nor eyewitnesses,
nor to be reassured by touch;

common sense –
here and now –
real presence
simply in the song.

Jan Sutch Pickard

'Camas is the Iona Community's outdoor activity centre on Mull. At Camas there is a strong focus on building community and connection; with each other and with our surroundings. Camas is home to a team of staff and volunteers who live down a two-kilometre track welcoming guests to share a simple way of life. The centre is housed in 200-year-old cottages which nestle in a beautiful bay on the Ross of Mull. The shore, garden and woodland provide an incredible setting for personal challenge and community growth.' (www.iona.org.uk)

REFLECTIONS

Jesus and the Justins

On Maundy Thursday in 2023, three elected officials – Rep. Justin Pearson of Memphis, Rep. Justin Jones of Nashville and Rep. Gloria Johnson of Knoxville – took to 'the well', or the floor, of the Tennessee State Legislature. They did so alongside thousands of children and young adults who had descended on the capitol to protest the legislature's unwillingness to address rampant gun violence across the country. The protesters were compelled to action after a shooting at a children's preschool in Nashville in which three children and three adults were murdered. This was my country's 128th mass shooting this year alone – at the time of writing, there have been 147 mass shootings across the country, in the 103 days of this year.

After a vote by the representatives, the two Justins, as they are now called, were expelled – both black men under the age of 30. Rep. Johnson, a white woman and retired teacher, avoided expulsion by one vote.

The irony of this injustice, perpetrated during our holiest week, was lost on no Christian. As I watched these events from my home in Tennessee, I saw plainly the trial of Jesus. The Republican-led legislature, stepping cleanly into the role of the Pharisees, took turns asking their highly specific questions in a vain attempt to trip up the prophets. With their bullhorns and civil unrest, the prophets themselves – one the son of a preacher, the other a former divinity-school student – threw over the tables of the money-changers while the temple leaders conspired against them. The parallels were so egregious that, frankly, I was somewhat impressed that Republicans remembered to yell 'Expel them!' rather than 'Crucify him!'

Thankfully, the Justins have now been returned to the legislature by the very people who first elected them. But the issues laid bare by this series of injustices – gun violence, ageism, the right of assembly, and blatant racism, among others – remain unresolved.

Perhaps, as members and associate members of the Iona Community, it is safe to assume that we stand alongside the Justins in their fight for common-sense gun reform in the United States. Not only do we likely agree politically, but also theologically. In this Easter season, when we read about those who put their hands in his wounds, and feasted with him over fish, we pray that we might be the kind of disciple who would recognise the Risen Christ when he stands right in front of us. In the Justins, we see that kind of Messianic witness, and with them, we lament the lack of responsible governance that has led to these 147 mass murders.

And yet it is not enough to bemoan the issues of gun violence in the USA. The real issue at the heart of this injustice is racism. Without the impacts of racism, white gun enthusiasts would have fewer enemies, fewer threats, fewer reasons to 'defend' themselves. Dr Jonathan Metzl, professor at Vanderbilt University in Tennessee and author of *Dying of Whiteness: How the Politics of Racial Resentment Is Killing America's Heartland*, argues that the intensity of the U.S. gun debate is best understood in the context of white privilege: *'Who gets to carry a gun in public? Who is coded as a patriot, and who is coded as a threat, a terrorist, or a gangster? What it means to carry a gun, own a gun, or buy a gun – those questions are not neutral. We have a history of defining that in very racial terms.'*[1]

Therefore, we will never effectively address gun reform unless, and until, we dismantle the structures of white privilege that make gun culture possible. Those privileges are not confined to the United States, or to conservative Christian cultures that feel alien to many of us. Sadly, white privilege extends even into the very institutions and organisations we love and support, and that includes the Iona Community itself. Our commitments to hospitality, worship and justice are all influenced by the overwhelming whiteness of our community. To be faithful Easter people, and effective at achieving any of our shared goals, we must critically assess our words, prayers and priorities, even in instances where we feel profoundly uncomfortable doing so, and challenge structural racism within our own community. The ability to walk away from that discomfort is itself an expression of privilege.

It is far too easy to stand in judgement of the unabashed culture of gun violence in the United States. As supporters of the Justins, as followers of Jesus, and as members and friends of the Iona Community, we must commit to challenging racism – even when it threatens the foundations of our most cherished temples.

Stacy Smith

Note:

1. From an interview in the *Guardian*, 9 August, 2019

My foot-washing teacher

Jesus, knowing that the Father had given all things into his hands and that he had come from God and was going to God, got up from supper, took off his outer robe, and tied a towel around himself. Then he poured water into a basin and began to wash the disciples' feet and to wipe them with the towel that was tied around him. He came to Simon Peter, who said to him, 'Lord, are you going to wash my feet?'

John 13:3–6 (NRSV)

After 27 years of living in Asia, I am often struck by the fact that the Bible is an Asian book. As I live among the Taiwanese, I see how the culture of this continent has shaped the culture of the Bible. Jesus was Middle Eastern, not Western, and he lived in an eastern culture.

The story of Jesus washing his disciples' feet on the last night of his life is told from an Asian perspective. Peter is an Asian student who knows that his teacher should not be washing his feet. Often Taiwanese Christians will describe themselves as students of Jesus. So, Peter protests and Jesus understands his protest by saying, 'You do not know now what I am doing, but later you will understand.' It is hard to break out of our cultural view. But Jesus constantly breaks through the view of the world and brings in a new culture, the culture of God's Kingdom.

This is a beautiful story because it once again shows the freedom of Jesus. We are told that 'Jesus, knowing that the Father had given all things into his hands and that he had come from God and was going to God, got up from supper, took off his outer robe, and tied a towel around himself. Then he poured water into a basin and began to wash the disciples' feet and to wipe them with the towel that was tied around him.' Hierarchy and status were of great importance in Jesus' Asian culture, just as they are equally important today. One of the worst things in Taiwan is to 'lose face'. You don't want anyone to look down on you. But because Jesus knew who he was as a beloved child of God, because he knew that God had put all things into his hands, because he knew that he would be returning to his place of honour in heaven, he was free to do the work of a servant. He shattered Asian cultural norms by kneeling and washing the feet of his students.

When we know who we are as beloved children of God, we are also free to serve with joy and abandon. When we know that our eternal destiny is in God's hands, we don't have to worry about our status. Our status does not come from how many people like our posts on social media, but our status, our worth comes from the God who creates us and redeems us and loves us with an unconditional love.

Peter needed his world view shattered. He spent his days with Jesus, but most of the time he did not understand this Kingdom which Jesus was ushering in. Peter's value system was shaped by Asian culture, but Jesus is a firm teacher, 'If I don't wash your feet, you can't be part of what I am doing.' If you hold on to the old world view, you can't walk in my way and love with my love. And Peter, with all of his shortcomings, is open to change. 'Not just my feet, but wash my head and my hands too!'

Jesus is a wonderful teacher, because he doesn't just tell his students what they should do, he models a new way of living and being and loving. So, he, their teacher and Lord, kneels and does the job of a servant.

One Holy Week I designed a Maundy Thursday service for our community at Taiwan Theological Seminary. The students in my preaching class were the leaders of this service. When it came time for the foot-washing, I had asked an indigenous student named Isa to wash the feet of his classmate. The liturgy for this service was abundant, and I was paying attention to the time. If worship services in the chapel are too long, I will hear about it.

But as Isa knelt to wash his classmate's feet, he was in no hurry. He poured the water over the feet and slowly washed them. He not only washed them; he began to massage them. He lovingly caressed the feet of his classmate, seemingly oblivious to the time or the rest of us in that chapel. I was transfixed and said to myself, 'Here is your teacher of how to wash feet in the name of Jesus.' In the past, I had poured water and then casually dried the feet of the one I was serving. But Isa gave me a new vision. 'Whatever you do, do it with love.'

Now when I was wash feet, I am never in a hurry. I do it in the name and spirit of Jesus. My student became my teacher, which has happened more times than I can remember.

Of all the things Jesus could have done on the last night of his life, like healing the sick or giving one more Sermon on the Mount, he chooses to kneel and wash the feet of his friends. I've often thought that foot-washing should be one of our sacraments, for Jesus told us to do it, just as he had done it. And when we do it, we are changed into the likeness of Jesus, who served with such freedom because he knew that he was loved by God and would return to God. As children of this same God, we can serve with that daring freedom. We can, as the hymn says, 'be lost in wonder, love, and praise',[1] as I was when I saw the way Isa washed his classmate's feet.

John McCall

Note:

1. From 'Love divine, all loves excelling', by Charles Wesley

Stay awake, and wait

I've never been very good at truly experiencing Easter, living out Lent and the Easter story. Life, ironically, gets in the way. Deadlines and exams loom, and I'm easily distracted by the imminent arrival of summer, as the sun shines and days get ever longer. This feels in contrast to Advent, in which, I feel, there is nothing much else to do, except wait. The days are short, and the nights are cold. Nothing to do except sit and witness the story unfolding. Yet, to deliberately draw out and mark the days, with summer so tantalisingly close, strikes me as the last thing I want to do.

And last year was no exception. I've never been one for fasting, or giving something up in Lent either. No way to bookmark the start of this holy period. And so, before I knew it, it was Holy Week, and I felt wholly unaware, and unequipped to celebrate. It was Maundy Thursday, and I was having dinner with some friends when we decided, rather impromptu, to attend a Church of Scotland service down the road. As we walked over, we joked about feeling rather apprehensive about the washing of feet, feeling rather uncomfortable about the prospect. Not for us, we thought. Not today, as ill-prepared as we were.

And yet, fast forward an hour, and we found ourselves, as though in a trance, all compelled to tenderly take our socks and shoes off, and advance, barefoot, down the cold slabs of the church. As the minister stooped low beneath me and tenderly washed my feet, I, too, along with the altar and church surrounding me, felt stripped. Stripped of the hard exterior we put on to cope with the world we live in, of the colourful clothes, bells and whistles we incorporate to keep us entertained, distracted and moving forward. Nothing to do but to sit in the vulnerability, and allow this man I didn't even know to kneel and tend the feet that have trodden a thousand miles.

After the altar had been stripped, people slowly processed out into the darkness, until there were just a handful of people huddled at the back around some candles. I don't remember making a decision to stay, but I found myself, now alone, among them.

Stood there, in the dark and silence, with nothing to do except witness the hours of the Easter story unfold, I felt utterly crippled. There were no distractions now. Nothing to do but stay awake, and wait. To sit there in the fear and dark, feeling utterly alone and helpless, and feel everything that the world never lets us feel.

I found myself crying. Crying as I surrendered myself to the fears of today. Climate chaos. The utter hopelessness I felt about this beautiful earth we inhabit. The fear of escalating violence and oppression inevitably to come, as we become more scared and fearful of one another and the world. The loss and devastation to wildlife: my friends, who over years became known by name to me – the curlew and the kittiwake. Nothing to tear me away from this grief. Nothing to do but sit, wait and stay awake. Bearing witness to these crimes. Watching and praying with Jesus. Waiting with him, as he surely must have felt the same grief, loneliness and desperation.

But, for the first time, understanding that my only task there in that moment was not to scramble for good news, not to diffuse the tension, not even to act. But instead to simply sit with Jesus. To stay present to the utter terror that was to come. How can we expect ourselves to change things if we cannot even acknowledge and grieve its happenings?

There are not enough spaces in our lives that allow for this witness. For many, the prospect of it is unthinkable, and we fear we will be plunged into despair so deep, there will be no way back. And yet, we believe … that in just three days, something just as unthinkable will happen. He will rise again! But if we are to experience such an act, we must too bear witness, as Jesus did, to the pain and mourning that comes before.

The Easter story that year gave me a unique gift I had never appreciated before, that my faith gives me in the context of this cruel, crucifying and crucified world. How every year, we must sit and wait, in darkness and uncertainty, and yet believe he will rise again. There is always light of hope, but that hope only lives if we allow ourselves to witness and feel the darkness first.

Eve Sharples

Bridging the gap

Jimi Calhoun writes from Bridging Austin, a reconciling community and inter-denominational church in Texas where he and his wife, Julaine, are pastors. Bridging is especially committed to welcoming those on the margins ...

Some people today wonder if the hippie values of peace, love and community from the mid-twentieth century are still relevant? I am a genuine San Francisco hippie who came into young adulthood in the late 1960s. My band rehearsed four blocks from the epicentre of 'hippiedom', the Haight-Ashbury district. Scott McKenzie sang a song that said 'If you come to San Francisco, summertime will be a love-in there.'[1] Yes, peace and love was in the air, but most were unaware that, at one time, San Francisco had made it illegal for 'any person who is diseased, maimed, mutilated, or in any way deformed, so as to be an unsightly or disgusting object ... to expose himself or herself to public view'.[2] It is Bridging Austin's mission to dispel the notion that a person's appearance – related to race or being differently-abled, or anything – disqualifies them from inclusion. The first question we had to ask ourselves when we began was how?

The answer came in the form of three words attributed to the English mystic Julian of Norwich. At one point she had become very ill and was at death's door. A priest was present at her bedside to comfort her in her transition but comfort was not what she sought. Her desire was to suffer with Jesus. Then a vision of the crucified Christ appeared to her. Julian referred to this experience as being 'disabled by Christ'[3] and she was able to equate her suffering with that of Christ's. In her physical limitations she felt a need to share in the burdens of another person, Jesus. For us, the question was: how could we emulate Julian and share in the sufferings of others, especially those excluded because of race or being differently-abled, and then bring health and healing to them?

Julian's illness caused her to have physical limitations and we knew there were many among us who were experiencing social limitations. There are those who tend to avoid people who make them uncomfortable when it comes to race and disability. To counteract this, we created a community rooted in empathic activism. To engage in activism of this type, it is necessary to see the world through lenses that do not reduce people to their skin colour or disabilities. In order to accomplish that, we apply 'empathetic imagination' by considering every issue from the other's point of view and then work backwards from there. It works like this: if you desire intimacy with others, then assume they do too. If you want to be appreciated purely for being you, then assume that they do. Now imagine how your life would be if your appearance prevented you from having access to those things.

In order to advance our mission at Bridging, we draw a distinction between being an inviting community and a welcoming community. This is why: the typical church in our area sets its ministry agenda according to the preferences of the congregation, or the capabilities of the staff. But a welcoming community plans with the other in mind. The following parable is one I frequently use to illustrate what it means to welcome someone Bridging-Austin-style.

Imagine that you are the largest cattle rancher in the state of Texas. Your daughter has been in California for the past two years, attending the University of California, Berkeley. For those of you unfamiliar with the geography, Berkeley is located about fifteen miles from San Francisco. And true to the region's recent past, it is a bastion of progressive activism. If you know anything at all about Texas, then you know Texas is a polar opposite in terms of political leanings.

You decide you want your daughter to come home for Christmas. As an added incentive, you tell her that you will send the family jet to fly her and any friends she'd like to invite to the family ranch. What you are not aware of is that during her time away she has embraced a vegan diet, and every one of the friends she is bringing is a vegan too. You slaughter your most prime beef to prepare the best meal possible. Your invited guests arrive but no one eats. You are perplexed and offended. Why are they abstaining after you have given them the best of everything? Jesus might have answered you this way, 'You did well to invite them, but since you did not consider their preferences first, you did little to welcome them.'

Bridging Austin is a welcoming community because we exist for the sake of the other, whoever that might be. We believe that every human being is part of a majestic work of art by the Creator God. Though all parts are not exactly the same in form or function, all parts owe their existence to the hand of the Creator and are worthy of dignity, respect and love. We exist to extend the love we have for Jesus to everyone who desires it, no exceptions!

We see the world as a spiritual place and our style of worship reflects that core belief. We desire to provide the opportunity for people to enjoy a meaningful spiritual experience by incorporating artistic elements such as painting, music, sacred silence, poetry, film, as well as traditional liturgical elements. Our services are designed to facilitate a spiritual conversation and we believe that we are here to learn from each other, valuing and welcoming thoughtful dialogue.

www.bridgingaustin.org

Jimi Calhoun

Notes:

1. By John Phillips, see www.songfacts.com

2. See https://en.wikipedia.org/wiki/Ugly_law

3. From *Disability in the Christian Tradition*, Brian Brock and John Swinton, William B. Eerdmans Publishing Co., 2012

Second Class Citizens

Stef Benstead knew first-hand how badly the UK was treating disabled people. She lived the truth herself, and heard similar stories the more people she spoke to.

Stef knew it was time to speak up, so in 2019 she wrote her book, *Second Class Citizens*, highlighting the wrongs and calling for a better way.

Stef's motivation comes in part from her faith, in part from a desire to improve the lives of other people, and in part from a knowledge that things can be done in better, more dignified ways. She's seen that herself, through the Manchester Poverty Truth Commission, of which she is a part.

In her book, Stef writes that the goal of a modern society should be that sick and disabled people have as much access as possible to the same choices as everyone else, in terms of where to live, work or study, and what to eat, wear and do. That ideal has been hamstrung by the removal of support systems and flawed attempts to improve the system, often arising above all from a failure to consult and listen to people with first-hand insight.

Dignity, agency and power in this context are inseparable.

Stef says: 'The importance of dignity is that it gives you back your self-worth. So often, people in poverty don't have control over a lot of events around them. I'm on sickness benefits and I get reassessed every two years and I don't have control over whether I'm going to have enough money to live off for the next two years or not.

'People might be in private rental housing and they don't have control over whether their landlord will come and make repairs for them or not. Or they're looking for work and they can't force an employer to offer them a job; they may be getting repeated rejections.

'A lot of these situations can be very demoralising and they can strip away your confidence in yourself and in your ability to change your future, because you quite often don't have a huge amount of ability to control your future. A dignified system would start from the assumption that people want to work where they can, and want to contribute, and the role of the state would be to enable that.

'The Poverty Truth Commission brings you into a situation where you can make a change because you are talking to the people who have decision-making power and they are listening because they want to learn, and it's dignified. Nobody thinks less of you because you are poor or are struggling or have been homeless. Instead, people recognise that you have some expertise, skills and knowledge that we all need.

'That gives you the power again that most people have over a substantial part of their life, where you can make a difference in your own life but also in the lives of other people, so you know you are making a difference in the world. You are helping other people's lives to be better, which everyone wants to do.

'Humans are social creatures; we like to help one another out. Part of poverty is not just that you can't support yourself; it's not being able to help other people either because you're so restricted in your own finances, your own time, your own resources. That is a really horrible place to be in. So to have people listen to you, to take you seriously, to implement your suggestions, to actually want to give you some control and give you the decision-making power, that's a really wonderful experience.'

Drawing on her faith, Stef adds: 'Every person has been created by God and that's what gives us our dignity. Part of how we worship God is how we live lives that display God's character to other people, and part of God's character is a massive concern for people in poverty, and therefore, one of the things that Christians are called to do, to worship God and to serve him, is to stand up for people in poverty, stand up against injustice and work for change so that poverty can be eradicated.

Church Action on Poverty and Stef Benstead

The Big One

Earth Day is 22nd April. In 2024, Earth Day comes just before the start of Holy Week, which seems appropriate. (Ed.)

'George Monbiot: Marry me', 'Unite To Survive', '4 Today And I'm Marching For My Future' – the messages and challenges shown in XR's action The Big One, from 21st- 24th April, 2023, were many, varied and very creative.

Over 200 organisations – from Greenpeace to CAFOD, CND to Scientists for Global Responsibility, the PSU to Quakers in Britain, Keep Britain Tidy to Avaaz – and the Iona Community – gathered together in and around Westminster to express their concern about the increasing seriousness of the climate emergency – and the need for action. Every major government department was picketed with messages specific to their areas of responsibility for having added to greenhouse gas emissions – and for their responsibility for now reducing them. This gave a very clear picture of how intersectional and indivisible the issues in this crisis are.

On the Saturday, Earth Day, there was a biodiversity march of thousands: both humans and many animals, insects, birds and marine creatures. I spent the day dressed as one of a trio of badgers, and it was a revelation to me how beloved and photogenic badgers are! I had my furry nose stroked by many small children and my picture taken by multiple photographers, both on mobile phones and large press cameras. We were raising awareness of the threat to biodiversity that the current ecological circumstances pose.

On Sunday there were worship services, and then a march to the Home Office, where many thousands of pink-paper origami boats were launched in a moat with a letter that could be sent either to Suella Braverman or to the writer's own MP addressing an upcoming debate in the House of Commons. The letter emphasised the significant effect that the climate emergency is already having on migration and the likelihood of a considerable increase in people needing to leave their homes as the effects of climate changes accelerate. I know just how *many* boats there were, as I spent the couple of days following The Big One in a team of people unfolding them, drying them out and collating them into piles to be sent to the MPs!

On the final stage of the action, in Parliament Square on Monday afternoon, after a day of sunshine – black clouds suddenly appeared and there was a heavy downpour – we quite expected a dramatic clap of thunder and a lightning strike of the Houses of Parliament!

About thirty Iona Community members took part in The Big One: picketing, marching, singing and praying ...

Despite the enormous amount of organisation it took to mount this action, the amazing amount of energy, creativity and sheer determination displayed before and after the action, and its duration, there was sadly almost no reporting of it by national media. The BBC's coverage was particularly disappointing.

However, this will not deter XR – we are already planning our next action. As António Guterres said at the opening of COP27: *'We are in the fight of our lives ... our planet is fast approaching tipping points that will make climate chaos irreversible. We are on a highway to climate hell with our foot on the accelerator.'* And from the IPCC's most recent report: *'Our world needs climate action on all fronts: everything, everywhere, all at once.'*

One participant movingly said this about the Big One:

> *'I think one great thing about this event is the possibility that it acted in the way an ecosystem builds – creating thousands of tiny little links between people and organisations as species build links with other species until they collectively become a whole ecosystem, where thousands of species live their different lives in interdependence with each other, collectively helping to create something bigger than any of them – a forest, a society. It's what we need – ecosystems of action where people play different yet complementary roles and ideally start to govern themselves without all this political party nonsense. It's empowering. Given the right circumstances a group of ordinary folk will come up with much better policies than any government ...'*

Margery Toller, 2023

A time of blessings

This reflection by Peter Millar is from 'A candle in the window', Peter's monthly e-mail of 'words to encourage in these times' which he has been sending out to friends around the world for several years now. Peter's reflection, from 2022, touches on many Holy Week and Easter themes, such as our shared humanity, and Christ's light and hope. (Ed.)

In January of 2016 I was diagnosed with incurable, but treatable, cancer in the bone marrow and this reality has been my long-term daily companion. Since 2016, I have always been on medication of one kind or another, except when I was very ill with Covid in 2021. Amazingly, given how sick I was, I have not so far had long Covid, but being off the cancer medicines did reactivate the 'multiple myeloma' (the official name for this type of cancer).

Since then it has been a fairly difficult pathway on various chemo rotations. I am once again on tough chemo treatment but it may be a while before the wonderful folk at the Western General Hospital, close to my home here in Edinburgh, will know if it is effective in any way.

However, in this reflection I do not intend just to relate a tale about all my cancer medicines. Living with this illness for almost seven years has taught me many rich lessons – perhaps some of which I could have done without, but also many others which I have valued greatly. Without sounding trite, overall it has been a time of blessings. But also I know that many people with cancer do not view it this way, and I understand from my experience in the oncology wards that there are multiple ways in which we respond to a cancer diagnosis.

For everyone in the world with cancer there is a hugely dynamic, often very difficult and lonely journey going on inside – in hearts and minds, for it is often a pathway rich in uncertainty. That basic truth can propel some amazingly rich and good human beings to take their own lives. It can also turn selfish and self-satisfied individuals into secular saints. It can break a family apart, and it can also wonderfully and surprisingly restore family life. It can lead in many homes to poverty and other related hardships. It can bring tears beyond number, and it can bring huge amounts of light and laughter, even on dark days. It can draw out vast wells of love and compassion, and it can draw out hate and bitterness and absolute despair. Why me?

It can lead to a quick death, and it can lead to a long slow dying. It demands inner strengths we never knew we had and it can also take them away. And everyone on this now very common journey is on a different road and with a different understanding of the illness and its implications. And it remains a truth within medical care in the rich parts of our world that millions of people who have been diagnosed with some type of cancer can be healed and millions cannot be. The level of cancer research now going on in our world is beyond our imagination. This important and prophetic research work is truly a marker of our times, of our corporate wisdom, of the dedication of thousands of people and a clear demonstration, if one is needed, that the forces of evil are not having it all their own way in our tumbling world.

Every day during this illness I have been grateful for all the medical care available from the fantastic National Health Service in the UK. No such level of treatment is present in many, many countries and for all of us this is another reality within the never-ending struggle for global justice. There is no level playing field in the world of global medicine and it is marginally hopeful that this urgent and particular concern, as with climate change, is being addressed in imaginative and creative ways by some governments, by aid agencies and by charitable foundations. We must never close our eyes and ears to the signs of hope, for they are at work.

During my life my spiritual explorations, and the writings which have emerged from them, have been framed by an understanding of the Christian faith which believes that the gospel message rings true when it is embedded in the amazing, often irritating, certainly uncertain life of our world. It is the knowledge that Christ's light and hope is at work in the daily grind. This is not in any way to denigrate the vital ministry of the World Church which daily brings strength and purpose to millions of our sisters and brothers, not least to those in poverty and struggle. I know from my own experiences overseas what the church means to people who are the 'hidden ones' in this world.

But when cancer became my companion at the age of 72, there were many other spiritual insights which were framing my response to the news. I have always been interested in the great religious traditions in the world and have lived alongside many people of other faiths. Over the years I have always written about my understanding of secularism and the many articulations of contemporary humanism. My cancer, and what goes on inside me each day because of it, has confirmed in me the hope that we are all humanists at heart, in the fullest meaning of that word, and that our humanism is embedded in a living faith. By that word 'faith' I mean that we live and move and have our daily being on planet Earth, encompassed in the knowledge that there is an Ultimate Reality at work, both in ourselves and in the natural world which is the source of all life. As the late Shirley Erena Murray in New Zealand wrote so powerfully in one of her wonderful hymns:

> *God of all living, God of all loving,*
> *God of the seedling, the snow and the sun,*
> *Teach us, deflect us,*
> *Christ re-connect us,*
> *Using us gently, and making us one.*[1]

What a visionary and inspiring grouping of wisdom from Shirley, with whom I had the privilege of sharing with many years ago. And that leads me to say that an incurable cancer, rooted in both the knowns and the unknowns of this life, has made me much more aware, than before, that each day is precious in a way that I find difficult to describe. Each day brings new possibilities of 're-connecting' in a life-giving way (surprising as it may seem) with the world, with others, with myself, with Dorothy who died in an instant in the arms of my son Tim and myself 21 years ago, and my children and grand-children (even though they are not living locally). And with friends around the world to whom I feel close even if they are far away.

I think of my days differently now, and accept what they offer in a new way. In terms of my mind and emotions, I don't run away from being depressed and anxious and bad-tempered and generally not a 'nice' person on some days. I am often lonely, even when surrounded by the love of family and friends, because cancer by its nature can be a lonely path. I am often bewildered by all that is going on in the world, yet in the same moment can feel streams of compassion flowing into my body from the nurses in haematology as I lie back allowing the chemo to wander through my system. And then half an hour later I ask myself do I really need to go through all of this at this stage. Certainly cancer allows, or rather propels, your emotions to run riot. But thankfully not 24/7!

This year in particular has been a roller coaster, marked most days by highs and lows and in betweens. It is the same for many others. We hold on. We speak to a friend. We phone the hospital. We may pray or watch TV or have a warm bath (despite the energy costs!). We may take some wine (I actually don't because I feel dreadful afterwards!). We think or we don't think. We worry and then suddenly all can be calm.

And we say more than once to ourselves where no one else hears it – is that another lump? Does that pain in my left shoulder mean the cancer is moving? How long have I got? Why won't my right arm move and why is my left leg all numb? Where is that pill I had in my hand a moment ago? (It has fallen on the floor and I can't reach it!) Why can't I go to beautiful Greece for a week? (Because you can't, and anyway it is far too hot for you there.) And so it goes on. Millions know what I mean. The muddled thinking and doing of the man on chemo! I hope it causes you to laugh for certainly it does for me. Perhaps I now just accept we are all muddled at one time or another, with or without cancer. And what is also true is that modern drugs, brilliant as they are vis-à-vis cancer treatments, have certain downsides for patients in terms of one's mind, behaviour and emotions. Many medics would agree with this.

When I sit quietly and listen to music and reflect, I feel, although it is difficult to write about it, that I am a better and more insightful human being than I was prior to my cancer journey. It is in that sense that in the latter part of this journey I can say that I am truly blessed. There will be pain and more difficult days ahead but these times will, I pray, awaken me to a deeper solidarity with all who suffer and hope in our beautiful wounded world.

Sooner or later, the bone marrow in me will no longer be able to bring health to my body. From dust we came, and to dust we return. But on the journey ahead, and while I am still conscious, I hope, as the poet R.S. Thomas said, that *there will be nights that are so still that I can hear the small owl calling ... and the swell born somewhere in the Atlantic rising and falling ... wave on wave on the long shore.*[2] And experience of the deep love of family and friends.

Thinking of you all and sending love and a prayer, Peter.

Peter Millar, 2022

Notes:

1. From 'Touch the earth lightly', by Shirley Erena Murray, Hope Publishing, 1992

2. From 'The Other', by R.S. Thomas, Collected Poems, W&N, 1985

I will not give up hope

We've heard of war, violence, inhuman cruelty, the death of civilians, the death of children, the destruction of the land and the suffering of animals in Ukraine for months now. As a Ukrainian student said at one of the vigils at the University of Edinburgh: 'It feels like it has been years already.'

A Latvian colleague, Leva, returned from an international conference recently and told of the shock and perplexity of many Western people there: 'We don't understand! We don't understand!''But we do,' she said. We have been living in the shadow or in the clutches of the same violator for centuries, in living memory, in the form of the Soviet Union.

The deepest problem is that Russia has never really reflected on its past (not like Germany after World War Two, for example). The crimes of occupation, oppression, deportations, genocide, greed and abuse of power have not been recognised.

Allow me to tell you just a bit about it. This is my story ...

When I was a child, May 9th was one of the most celebrated days of the year. 'Day of the Victory' it was called (not the end of WWII). Masses were gathered in huge military parades – with flags, tanks, guns, icon-like pictures of Communist Party leaders (rather curious in an officially atheist country) and colourful, floating balloons. The balloons were the only positive thing for me as a little girl.

We were forced to go. If we hadn't, my mother would have got into serious trouble, and would have had to answer in front of the Party. So we went and bore the cheerfulness and the show of the military power of the oppressor. The balloons floated on my ceiling for several days afterwards, which was a tiny compensation.

As a child, I knew this was an oppressor ... because the very closest friends of my family had died in Siberia. They were farmers, humble and cheerful people doing their work, welcoming others, sharing a joke or two with my family – that's how I knew them – and, well, simply living. They hadn't done anything wrong. They were three brothers, the youngest of them being somewhat disabled. He was the only one of the three who had married.

One day he was at a market in town doing some business and enjoying the diversions of it from country life. When he came home at night, all the doors of their farmhouse were open and his whole family was gone: his wife, his brothers. He asked around in despair and sorrow, and heard that there were some cattle trains full of people at the station. He went there to look for his family, but was pushed away. He then volunteered to get on a train, in hope of finding them. They squeezed him in. But he never saw his dear ones again – he died on the way – as many others did, standing for weeks with no food or water in a train meant for cattle, on the way to labour camps in Siberia. His brothers died of cold and hunger in the camps. Only his wife returned, decades later, a broken and bitter woman.

I knew this was an oppressor ... because I was living in the divided garden of my great-grandfather. We were lucky to be allowed to stay in the house at all. My great-grandfather was a man from a very poor family. He'd worked and worked, saved and saved – and had bought a bit of land on the out-skirts of the town. Each window and each door of that house looked different, because they were all second-hand. We were worried that the roof wouldn't hold in the autumn storms, because the beams he had used to secure it were so thin and worn.

He gave the ground floor to the Jewish school, most of the rooms to tenants, and kept working, repairing shoes for people, and saving for some orchard trees. They were his pride and joy! And then, all of them were taken away – his painstakingly and lovingly planted orchard given to settlers.

His only two children were separated for life. His daughter, my grandmother, stayed in Latvia, while his son was forced to escape to America. He was also somewhat disabled and therefore only got called into the army in the very last days of the war. It happened to be the German one (armies moved back and forth over the Latvian land the whole time). Many brothers, fathers and sons were forced to fight on opposite sides.

The brother, Paulis, and sister, Velta, only met once more in life, after more than 50 years of separation, but the father, Janis, never saw his son again. And he only saw his orchard again through someone else's fence.

I knew this was an oppressor ... because in the 1980s I went to the military zone in the west side of Latvia. It was there to keep people confined to the

Soviet with no way to escape. For many did try to escape – in tiny boats on the sea, in homemade flying machines. They were caught and killed or deported. And the whole zone became a military machine. I remember the mud left after the tanks had driven through it, the smell of chemicals, the abandoned houses with windows staring like empty eyes and a rope with a loop swinging from a dead tree like a gallows. I was just a child, but I never forgot that. Military powers are destructive – for people, for the land, for the environment.

I knew this was an oppressor ... because I had to go to a violent, oppressive school especially made for the Russification of my people.

I knew this was an oppressor ... because Russian-speaking strangers on the trolleybus kept telling me, a child: 'Just you wait, we will send you all to Siberia!'

I knew this was an oppressor – and I risked my life for freedom and independence from the Soviet.

When I was 14, I joined the Underground Church. Our group was literally underground – we met in a cellar underneath a church in Riga. There Rev. Aida Predele, an ordained minister in the Latvian Lutheran Church, talked to us about the Christian faith. She told us about God's unconditional love and about our call to work for peace rooted in justice. That was exactly what I was looking for! I wanted something to give meaning to my life, to sustain me through the toughest times. I was also looking for Someone to love me and the world, the environment I had grown to love so much myself. My Grandmother Velta was travelling around Latvia playing the organ throughout all the dangerous Soviet times. As a girl I went with her, and one time – standing in front of an altar of a tiny countryside church – I had a profound experience of being loved deeply and unconditionally. I wanted to learn about what that was!

In the cellar underneath the church I came to understand more. Aida also encouraged me to pursue theology studies, when the faculty opened again after Latvia gained independence.

In the Underground Church, many of us went on the barricades, joined the Baltic Chain, kept up messages of hope and resistance. During the barricades the churches in the centre of Riga were turned into hospitals for the wounded and places of rest for the tired. We were singing and praying in the bitter cold of January – together, all faiths and none. And we won! The Baltic States are free and independent. And the youth of the Underground Church are free to live their faith openly; most of us have become ministers in diverse denominations and in one case, a nun.

And that's just a tiny bit of the whole story ...

I want to say: Wake up, Russia, wake up! Think, reflect, repent and change your ways! Ukraine is not Russia. Ukrainians have their own language, history and dignity. They have the right to live in their country in peace!

I'm afraid many people in Russia support Putin and are brainwashed with propaganda. Alternative sources of information have been blocked more and more in Russia over the past years. Protesting openly often ends in imprisonment and newspapers and radio stations that tell a different story have either been shut down or have moved out of Russia (several to Latvia).

But there are people who think differently, people who resist in diverse ways. Those who do not want to be part of what Putin is doing try to keep in contact with friends and colleagues in Europe and beyond. Many move away if they can. And some of those, who already live outside Russia, do wonderful things supporting refugees and people in need. Just recently I received a message from a Russian colleague saying: 'And I am packing Easter treats for Ukrainian families. Working as an Easter bunny today. Just got back from the house. There are around 18-20 families. Got treats for everyone and six traditional Easter cakes. And huge British Easter eggs. Many will go to church tonight, the majority will go tomorrow. My husband and I will celebrate with one of the families.' Things like that make my heart sing!

You might ask, 'Yes, but what can we do?' A lot!

1. Convince your government to take in refugees. Not only Ukrainians – any people in need and in danger. Tell them of compassion. Tell them that history also shows that many countries have benefited from doing this – it's a give and take, not only about being 'charitable'. We are all human and belong together.

2. Show solidarity. The Archbishop of the Latvian Evangelical Lutheran Church Worldwide, Lauma Zuševics, recently told of how the older people

in her community, who escaped after WWII, are now fearing that history is repeating itself. PTSD, flashbacks, nightmares return.

Yes, it is a similar time, but not quite the same. Then the whole world didn't hang out Polish flags. Then people couldn't agree on what to do. Now people stand in solidarity: sunflowers are planted all around the globe, Ukrainian flags are flown everywhere, vigils and protests held, help sent to Ukraine, to the refugees. Poorer countries like Moldova are still taking refugees in. Women and children in the Baltic States and Poland are weaving camouflage nets and making gift boxes for kids in the war zone. Latvia and Lithuania have offered cancer treatment for refugees.

3. Plant a sunflower and put it on the global map. See the website https://guerillapeaceukraine.org. The sunflower has become the symbol of solidarity, resistance, resilence, hope for peace and the end of the war in Ukraine. Sunflowers tell of life and the hope of new beginnings. They are literally life-giving, as they sustain pollinators, can be used to enrich the soil and are sustenance for many people and animals. Sunflowers are known for their heliotropism: they turn to face and follow the sun. They keep turning towards the light!

As I was walking to the Chaplaincy of Edinburgh University to lead a vigil, I noticed a different flower. A primula lying on the street. It was thrown out, roots, blossom, leaves, soil and all – light blue and yellow petals scattered on the ground for passers-by to trample. I walked past, but then turned back and picked it up. I'm getting many messages from friends and colleagues in the war zone and surrounding countries – day and night. People are saying: 'We have no hope left. Everything is getting destroyed. The cities will be rubble. People are dying on the streets.' Yes, that is true. But I refuse to give up hope! I refuse to leave the flower on the street to be trampled and die. I will take it, plant it, care for it. And maybe, just maybe, there will be a new beginning and hope will blossom again. I will not give up hope.

Urzula Glienecke, May 2022

Easter in Africa

The Iona Community is a global community and international movement, with members, associate members and Friends all across the world. They meet together in Family Groups and Regions, as well as online. They also work in close partnership with other ecumenical communities globally and together in different Common Concern Networks (see www.iona.org.uk).

There are over 30 associate members in Africa currently, living in Ghana, Kenya, Malawi, Burundi, the DRC, Tanzania and Uganda.

Some associate members in Kenya share the experience of Easter in Africa:

The Easter holiday is a time when Christians all over the world memorialise the sufferings, sacrifices and resurrection of Jesus Christ. In Africa, Easter is a spiritual celebration as well as a social one. Spiritually, it is a time when we are reminded of the freedom brought by Christ at Calvary. Socially, it is a time when many people get to slow down from their busy schedules and to gather with family and friends for relaxing times.

Generally, Easter in Africa involves a communal celebration, with different groups of people celebrating it differently, depending on their faith and beliefs, location and even financial abilities. People take pride in their traditions and make effort to keep them alive. Here are common traditions across the continent:

Rest

In Africa, Easter means a long weekend. A long weekend that comes just when most schools have closed for the holiday. It is the first public holiday of the year after New Year's, hence affording every one to take a breather from whatever keeps them busy. Most offices are closed, a good number of businesses also close down, that, with schools closing, means that people can take a few days of vacation. Some even plan their vacation time around this same time so that they can get extra days of vacation.

Fellowship and 'swallow-ship'

The long Easter weekend creates a perfect opportunity for families and friends to gather in large numbers. People travel from one end of the country to the other; some even cross borders so they can enjoy time with their loved ones. In some cases, the Easter holidays have replaced what used to happen during the December holidays. Groups of families and friends travel to a central location for a time of catching up. The mornings are lazy, the meals are sumptuous and the evenings are lively with many late nights.

Church services

Different churches have different activities leading up to the Easter holidays. During the 40 days of Lent, many believers have a time of repentance and reflection. Some take it a step further into a time of fasting, prayer vigils, and practices for whatever the church will be doing during Easter.

During the Easter holidays, going to a church service is the most fundamental undertaking for many Christians. Many will choose to attend a church service regardless of where they are. Even those travelling will schedule their travel plans in a manner that allows them to attend at least one service over the long weekend. Some churches run services from Thursday (the eve of Good Friday) through Sunday.

Easter plays

An emerging trend in some urban areas in Africa is Easter plays that take place both inside and outside of churches. While the stories at the beginning used to tell the Easter story, the plays have now evolved and matured to encourage believers to live upright lives and live well with their fellow people. Instead of just the reminder of what Jesus Christ did on the cross, there is also the challenge of living to be more like Jesus. The plays run for the duration of the Easter holiday; a good number of them having their 'premier shows' on Thursday. Over the years, the plays have been known even to attract audiences of non-Christians.

These are just a few of the Easter traditions over the continent of Africa. They have all evolved over time, informed by changing times and demands of different audiences. There are many more community-specific traditions that one will encounter, and those too are part of the Easter holiday tradition.

In work and worship,
God is with us.

Gathered and scattered,
God is with us.

Now and always,
God is with us.

Prayer from the Iona Community's daily 'office'

Winnie Nanjala, Mauryn Naliaka and Cindy Nekesa

A servant to others

Iona has always been a special place for me, having grown up visiting the Community on numerous occasions. So when the opportunity came to volunteer and, later in the year, live as a guest for Student Week, I simply could not turn either down.

In the spring of 2022, for two and a half months, I volunteered in the Iona Abbey kitchen. Within the first few days of being there, I was cooking main meals, soups for lunch and baking endless amounts of cakes, biscuits, flapjacks and puddings. The only previous experience I had was my own love of cooking and baking, and so the wonderful mentoring of Abbey Cook Anja and Assistant Cook Annie really helped improve my ability and expanded my knowledge of cooking for a variety of dietary requirements. The kitchen was such a relaxed and friendly working environment and, despite the early mornings, I really looked forward every day to working in the kitchen team.

I was presented with so many opportunities during my time with the Community: I was able to take part in worship, which included playing my tenor horn as part of the Easter services; I led morning worship a number of times; joined in the wee sing each Sunday afternoon; and was able to go on the pilgrimage round the island.

Living in community on Iona was like living with a constantly changing family, with both guests and volunteers coming and going. I made great friends with other volunteers and resident staff, spending many sunny days on beaches across the island, having fun playing frisbee, swimming, eating ice cream and even attempting to play golf on the machair. Several times, the volunteers from Camas came over to Iona, more friendships were made and this led to my first visit to Camas. A few of us headed there from Iona, stayed overnight at the Centre and joined in with sea kayaking the next morning. I was struck by what a beautiful location Camas is in and was very grateful for the opportunity to visit.

I really got the sense of island community through many different events, including Martyrs' Bay pub opening for the first time after the pandemic, and the opening of the new village hall, which included a ceilidh, open to all, which was so much fun and lasted into the early hours of the morning.

My time as a volunteer was such an amazing experience and had such an impact on me that when I knew I was returning as a guest for Student Week in September, I was eager to volunteer again in the kitchen the week before, to help cover staff holiday. The move between being a volunteer and then becoming a guest was however an interesting one! It felt strange to be served, rather than doing the serving and also to turn up to mealtimes without having been involved with the cooking!

Student Week was a great week, jointly led by the University of Glasgow and the Student Christian Movement (SCM) with Ashwin Africanus Thyssen of Stellenbosch University, the invited guest speaker.

The sessions throughout the week included talks on discipleship, the pilgrimage around the island, a trip to Staffa, an introduction to SCM, a wee sing and sessions on activism. It was a well-packed week but in the pockets of time between sessions, I enjoyed taking students who'd not been to Iona before to some of my favourite places, which included a climb up Dun I and a chilly September swim at Port Ban. It was so good to share the week and the different activities with other students from universities across the country. I really valued the time to be able to reflect and discuss how we live our lives through our faith, how we can be a servant to others and, through stewardship and activism, what changes we can make to have an impact on the world around us.

My time on Iona was amazing, inspiring and challenging all at the same time. I met so many brilliant people, created so many unforgettable memories and I am so thankful to have been able to spend time in such an incredible place – and can't wait to be back once again!

Peter Charman

For information on volunteering with the Iona Community, see www.iona.org.uk

A story from the road

When I left Iona after Easter week, I wondered if I'd ever meet Jesus again – in the 'real world'.

The week had been so powerful for me. The coming together of so many things in my time on Iona. In my life. Sitting in the cloisters and crying after the Maundy Thursday service – after Jesus was arrested, and the communion table was stripped and draped in black. The waiting in desolation and depression. And then, on Easter Sunday – Resurrection. Lighting candles at midnight and singing 'Christ Be Our Light'. Hugging everyone.

So Iona, for me, was a place where I finally started to face the issues in my life. Issues like abandonment, betrayal, death ... I started seeing patterns in my life, and in the life of the world. I began seeing how Jesus's story was, as they say, 'a story to live by'. Christ started to live in me. In my flesh and blood.

I was feeling down when I left the island, emotional – I hadn't felt that emotional in a long time. A real grief: leaving community and all we had shared living and working together. I felt wrung out, but hopeful. Vulnerable, but open.

I left with a group; we shared a meal on the ferry to Oban – bread and cheese and a thermos of tea – and did the morning office together. Then, gradually, we all went our separate ways: out into the world. All the witnesses – dispersed. We would keep in touch, we said. Write letters.

I had some tough times, some dead ends it seemed like. But I tried to remain hopeful and disciplined. Then it started to happen: I visited a man I knew who was living in a nursing home. He was talking to me. About his life. He'd had a stroke. He was writing everything down so that he could remember, he said – the names of things and the people who came to visit him. Still, life was good: he enjoyed the music appreciation and poetry evenings they had at the home, the good food. The view out back of the pine and cedar trees, evergreen scent with the windows wide and curtains dancing.

He was thankful, he told me, and smiled. It wasn't easy for him to smile: he'd lost control of the muscles all down one side of his face, all down one side of his heavy body. I was thinking to myself that it was pretty amazing – him smiling – and then, all of a sudden, in a flash, I recognised him as the Christ:

Christ on the cross. Christ, resurrected. He asked me about my time on Iona.

Talking to him, sitting with him there, healed me in a way.

I visited my folks. We had grown closer somehow. My mother told me things I never knew about her – things she had gone through growing up. She was telling me a story, and suddenly the lines in her face in the soft, late-evening light were beautiful: there was an agony in the garden traced there; but a sign of the resurrection somehow too.

Then I met a homeless man in London, in Euston station. We were talking intensely: about life, about suffering. But about how wonderful and mysterious and incredible life is too. We shared his bottle and my fish and chips between us. He had a very profound understanding – well, he'd been through a lot in his life. A lot of abandonment, betrayal, death … Every day I guess: waking up in the park, walking down the road into the city to be crucified by the state, by the crowds, by his self.

We were very honest with each other. He shared a poem he'd written; recited it by heart with his eyes closed. I started to cry, it was so beautiful. I can't say what it was about, exactly. It was the way he spoke and sang it. Something in his broken, scarred voice. In his transfigured, life-lined face. It was like the poem was light and resurrection above all the pain and suffering – all the pain and suffering in the world. I turned to thank him but he had gone, suddenly disappeared. I saw him later, walking ahead of me; shuffling and stumbling through the crowd at King's Cross station.

Sometimes I recognise Christ in moments like that. Other times, it's more in the everyday: sharing good news or lunch with a friend; turning and meeting a stranger's smile; in company of my partner as we journey along, or pause somewhere in the heart of silence – moments like that. I try to remain open to it. It's not always easy.

'Greetings,' I wrote to my Iona friend. 'Christ is risen! So, have you seen him?'

He responded, on a postcard of a city sunrise: 'Christ is risen! He is risen indeed! Yes.'

He's doing volunteer work. I'm getting ideas of going back to school – nursing maybe, community work? Terry is working midnights at a corner shop in Sheffield: it's not the job, he says, it's the people. The people who come in off the cold, mean streets; talking to them at all hours. Listening – if he can just learn to stay open, he says.

Julie is travelling. Last time Ray heard she was somewhere in South India. It's all a road, it's all a pilgrimage – life – wherever you are. I still feel we're all connected. Who knows, maybe we'll meet again one day.

I have moments sometimes when I can see light radiating and glancing off everything, everyone. It's like the light I witnessed on Iona: that beautiful, warm, amazing light falling, like God's glowing grace, on the Ross of Mull; shining on the sea.

They say that Iona is 'a thin place': a place where the separation between the material and the spiritual realm is only tissue-thin. It's tissue-thin everywhere I'm discovering: in India; in Euston Station; in hometowns; in lonely, desperate corner shops at drunken midnight ...

Everywhere, I want to cry, and shout, 'Hallelujah – yes!'

Neil Paynter

ABOUT THE CONTRIBUTORS

Stef Benstead is an independent researcher in disability and welfare. Her book, *Second Class Citizens* (2019), provides a history of the UK's treatment of disabled people and the creation and subsequent degradation of the welfare state. As someone dependent on benefits due to chronic illness, she is also an active participant in various Church Action on Poverty projects, and has a keen interest in Christian teaching on poverty and socio-economic justice.

Jimi Calhoun is a former world-class bassist who performed with several popular acts in the 1970s. Jimi's spiritual odyssey began with baptism in an American Baptist Church. He took up ordination with a Pentecostal denomination, then attended a Presbyterian Church, followed by reception into the Anglican Communion. He is the author of several books.

Julaine Calhoun was raised in the Roman Catholic tradition and later became part of the Calvary Chapel movement that spawned the Jesus People movement in the USA. She was a singer on a weekly Christian Television Programme in Los Angeles. In 1992 Julaine became a licensed minister followed by ordination. Julaine served in Belize City for eight years as a church planting missionary.

Martin Callam: 'I have lived in Norwich with my wife Paula since 1986. I have three adult children. I currently work as the Administrator for the Norwich Methodist Circuit and have nearly completed my training as a Local Preacher. I have been an associate member of the Iona Community since 2015.'

Paula Callam: 'I was born in the early 1950s in the north of England but grew up in Scotland, where I met and married Martin. We have three children and three grandchildren. We now live in Norwich, Norfolk. I have been a member of the Methodist Church since the '70s. I did short-term summer missions in Bosnia from 1998 to 2006. From 2008 to 2015 Martin and I coordinated the Street Pastors Initiative in Antigua and Barbuda. From 2016 I have been involved with a local charity that mentors prison leavers. I have been an associate member of the Iona Community since 2015.'

Peter Charman is a final year Radiotherapy and Oncology student at Glasgow Caledonian University, part of the Iona Community Student Group at the University of Glasgow and a member of the Methodist Church.

Church Action on Poverty: Poverty robs people of their dignity, agency and power. Church Action on Poverty works with a wide range of partners to build a movement in which people and communities can reclaim that dignity, agency and power together. You can find out more – and get involved – at www.church-poverty.org.uk

Alex Clare-Young is a member of the Iona Community and a URC minister, writer and activist. They are currently ministering as a pioneer minister in Cambridge City Centre, working with those who are at the margins of church and/or have challenges to offer the church. Alex teaches regularly and is an associate tutor at Westminster College, Cambridge.

Jo Clare-Young is a new member of the Iona Community and a minister and liturgist. They currently work as mission and training officer for the URC's Eastern Synod. Together, Jo and Alex have facilitated several programme weeks on Iona as part of their work with the Iona Community's LGBTQ+ Common Concern Network. They enjoy working together to facilitate worship, retreats and content that is accessible, relevant and refreshing. Jo and Alex are married and live in Cambridgeshire with their dogs Digger and Dharma, who enjoy taking their humans for a walk.

Margaret Crawshaw: 'I am a Methodist minister and an associate of the Iona Community who is passionate about justice issues. In retirement, I enjoy my grandchildren, walking and opportunities to be creative.'

Doug Dunlap has been an associate member of the Iona Community since the year 2000. He and his wife, Mary, live on an old Maine farm where, after many years of tending sheep, they now keep honeybees. Ordained in the United Church of Christ, he has served church and hospital chaplain ministries. Doug is engaging in a ministry to encourage people, young and old, to open themselves in turbulent times to the natural world, to discover its beauty, wonder, healing power and holiness.

Kathy Galloway is a writer and activist. A member and former Leader of the Iona Community, she is the author of a dozen books on justice issues, spirituality and poetry, and her writings have been widely anthologised. She lives in Glasgow.

Rev. Dr Urzula Glienecke is a Latvian theologian, artist and activist living in Scotland. She is a member of the Iona Community and is currently working as one of the chaplains at the University of Edinburgh. She has worked, studied and taught in Latvia, Norway, Germany, Spain, Republic of Ireland, Scotland and has travelled around the world. She is passionate about working together with people on the margins of society and preserving our diverse and wonderful environment.

Catriona Gorton is training to be an architect, with a particular interest in sustainable and heritage buildings. Her faith drives her commitment to sustainability and justice.

Fiona Gorton works for a human rights organisation and is treasurer and involved in eco-church for her Methodist church in the north-west of England. Since her teens, the Iona Community and its concerns have helped shape her faith and life.

Janet Killeen studied English and American literature, and taught in a London comprehensive school for over thirty years. She is an active member of her local Anglican church in South East London. She has published poems, short stories and two novels, and is a regular contributor to Wild Goose books.

Janet Lees is a member of the Lay Community of St Benedict. She blogs at https://foowr.org.uk/notesfrombambi/. She is the author of *Word of Mouth: Using the Remembered Bible for Building Community,* and *Tell Me the Stories of Jesus: A Companion to the Remembered Gospel* (Wild Goose Publications).

Emma Major is a pioneer lay minister, blind wheelchair user, artist and poet. She has written seven poetry books on disability, grief, mental health, faith and climate change. You can find Emma online at LLMCalling.com or on social media @emmuk74, where she shares her creativity to encourage, bless and affirm people.

John McCall, a longtime associate member of the Iona Community, has lived in Taiwan for over 25 years. In addition to teaching at Taiwan Seminary, he also accompanies and mentors Taiwanese pastors, who also accompany and mentor him.

Euan McPhee: 'I am an ecologist and former higher-education lecturer who taught environmental science. I have also cycled from Truro to Paris, Bonn and Glasgow for COPs 21, 23 and 26. Also, as a former smallholder, I devoted much time to practical conservation; I am currently Chair of the Friends of

Tregoniggie Woodland in Falmouth where I still get my hands dirty helping manage this public space. I am a Methodist Local Preacher.'

Peter Millar is a former Iona Abbey Warden and the author of several books, including *Finding Hope Again*, Canterbury Press, and *Our Hearts Still Sing*, Wild Goose Publications. He is a soul friend to many.

Mauryn Naliaka is an associate member of the Iona Community in Kenya.

Winnie Nanjala is an associate member of the Iona Community in Kenya.

Cindy Nekesa is an associate member of the Iona Community in Kenya.

Neil Paynter is an editor, writer and late-night piano player. Previously he worked in homeless shelters and nursing homes. He has worked for the Iona Community for about a quarter of a century.

Katharine M. Preston is lay eco-theologian, writing about issues of social justice, indigenous wisdom and climate change. She is the author of *Field with a View*, and co-editor with Kathy Galloway of *Living Faithfully in the Time of Creation*, both published by Wild Goose. Katharine lives with her husband, John Bingham, on a farm in Essex, New York. Both are active associates of the Iona Community, Katharine acting as the Coordinator for the Northeast USA region.

Christine Rowntree (79) born and educated in Edinburgh. Worked in Lesotho (volunteer), Essex, Malawi and Birmingham teaching science in local Secondary schools. Married to Simon with two grown-up daughters and twin granddaughters. I have been an Iona associate since the late 1980s.

Simon Rowntree: Born 1941. Married; two daughters, two twin granddaughters. Associate since 1980s. University administrator 1964–1995: Lesotho, Essex, Malawi, Aston (Birmingham).

Mark Scholefield has been living on Iona since 2019, listening to the wind and the waves and capturing glimpses of the island with pen and camera.

Eve Sharples, 23 years old, is a Young Adult member of the Iona Community, currently studying zoology at the University of Glasgow. She is involved in climate activism and interested in what our faith has to offer in this climate crisis.

Stacy Smith: After fourteen years of ministry in Memphis, Stacy Smith is now a 'travel pastor' in the Presbyterian Church (USA) and serves congregations in the midst of leadership transition. She is also a member of the Iona Community's Common Concern Network (CCN) on racism.

Jan Sutch Pickard: 'I am a former Vice President of the Methodist Church, a former Warden of the Abbey in Iona, a former Ecumenical Accompanier (peace monitor) in Palestine and Israel. But what am I now? A poet, storyteller and occasional preacher living on the Isle of Mull, a mother, grandmother and (I hope) good neighbour. And a child of God. Always.'

Margery Toller: Iona Community member. Four sons and a husband. In chaplaincy from newborns to hospice, further education to prison. Moderator of the Iona Community's CCN on Reconciliation, Peacemaking and Disarmament. Sometime gardener at Iona Abbey.

Westminster Presbyterian Church, Austin, Texas: In the summer of 2022, eleven teens and three adults from Westminster Presbyterian Church in Austin, Texas journeyed to Scotland to explore their Presbyterian heritage and deepen their faith. As part of their pilgrimage, they spent a week at Camas and had the opportunity to visit the Abbey and participate in worship. It just so happened that the worship leader, Stacy Smith, was an old friend of one of the group leaders! Stacy invited each member of the Westminster group to contribute a line for an eco-psalm that was read in evening worship.

Martin Wroe is married to Meg, a painter, and together they have been raised by three children. He fell into journalism while studying theology and ended up on the staff of the *Independent* and later the *Observer*. He has had longtime collaborations with the Greenbelt Arts Festival, the human rights NGO Amos Trust and the rock band U2. He contributes to BBC Radio 4's *Thought for the Day* and accidentally became a volunteer vicar in the Church of England. He was late to understand that religions are poems and tries to write one most days. His most recent book of poems is *Julian Of Norwich's Teabag* and, with Malcolm Doney, wrote *Hold On, Let Go*, a collection of daily readings about keeping your feet on the sacred earth and taking off. At the same time. Both books are published by Wild Goose.

SOURCES AND ACKNOWLEDGEMENTS

Passages from NRSV copyright 1989, Division of Christian Education of the National Council of the Churches of Christ in the United States of America. Used by permission. All rights reserved.

Pencil drawing of flower breaking through the hard earth (p.43), by Urzula Glienecke ©

A prayer for Ukraine, by Janet Lees, from *Coracle*: the magazine of the Iona Community, Neil Paynter (Ed.)

Sleepless, by Jan Sutch Pickard, from *Coracle*: the magazine of the Iona Community, Neil Paynter (Ed.)

Storm imminent, by Mark Scholefield, from *Coracle*: the magazine of the Iona Community, Neil Paynter (Ed.)

Your hurting, crying world, by Euan McPhee, from *Coracle*: the magazine of the Iona Community, Neil Paynter (Ed.)

For generations to come, by Christine Rowntree, from *Coracle*: the magazine of the Iona Community, Neil Paynter (Ed.)

Do we not hear?, by Douglas Dunlap, from *Coracle*: the magazine of the Iona Community, Neil Paynter (Ed.)

After Thomas, by Jan Sutch Pickard, from *Between High and Low Water: Sojourner Songs*, Jan Sutch Pickard, Wild Goose Publications, 2008

Jesus and the Justins, by Stacy Smith, from *Coracle*: the magazine of the Iona Community, Neil Paynter (Ed.)

Bridging the gap, by Jimi Calhoun, from *Coracle*: the magazine of the Iona Community, Neil Paynter (Ed.)

Second Class Citizens, by Church Action on Poverty and Stef Benstead, from *Dignity, Agency, Power: Stories, Prayers and Reflections from 40 Years of Church Action on Poverty*, edited by Niall Cooper, Chris Howson and Liam Purcell, Wild Goose Publications, 2022

The Big One, by Margery Toller, from *Coracle*: the magazine of the Iona Community, Neil Paynter (Ed.)

A time of blessings, by Peter Millar, from *Coracle*: the magazine of the Iona Community, Neil Paynter (Ed.)

I will not give up hope, by Urzula Glienecke, from *Coracle*: the magazine of the Iona Community, Neil Paynter (Ed.)

A servant to others, by Peter Charman, from *Coracle*: the magazine of the Iona Community, Neil Paynter (Ed.)

A story from the road, by Neil Paynter, from *Lent and Easter Readings from Iona*, Neil Paynter (Ed.), Wild Goose Publications, 2002, reprinted 2003, 2004, 2008

Wild Goose Publications, the publishing house of the Iona Community established in the Celtic Christian tradition of Saint Columba, produces books, e-books, CDs and digital downloads on:

- holistic spirituality
- social justice
- political and peace issues
- healing
- innovative approaches to worship
- song in worship, including the work of the Wild Goose Resource Group
- material for meditation and reflection

Visit our website at
www.ionabooks.com
for details of all our products and online sales